Edinburgh Lectures
on Mental Science

(1909)

Judge Thomas Troward

ISBN 0-7661-0749-3

THE EDINBURGH LECTURE SERIES

The
EDINBURGH LECTURES
ON MENTAL SCIENCE

BY

THOMAS TROWARD

LATE DIVISIONAL JUDGE, PUNJAB
AUTHOR OF "BIBLE MYSTERY AND BIBLE MEANING"

Fides et Amor Veritas et Robur

NEW YORK
ROBERT M. McBRIDE & CO.
1928

FOREWORD.

THIS book contains the substance of a course of lectures recently given by the writer in the Queen Street Hall, Edinburgh. Its purpose is to indicate the *Natural Principles* governing the relation between Mental Action and Material Conditions, and thus to afford the student an intelligible starting-point for the practical study of the subject.

T. T.

March, 1904.

THE WRITER
AFFECTIONATELY DEDICATES
THIS LITTLE VOLUME
TO
HIS WIFE

CONTENTS.

The Edinburgh Lectures on Mental Science.

I.

SPIRIT AND MATTER.

IN commencing a course of lectures on Mental Science, it is somewhat difficult for the lecturer to fix upon the best method of opening the subject. It can be approached from many sides, each with some peculiar advantage of its own; but, after careful deliberation, it appears to me that, for the purpose of the present course, no better starting-point could be selected than the relation between Spirit and Matter. I select this starting-point because the distinction—or what we believe to be such—between them is one with which we are so familiar that I can safely assume its recognition by everybody; and I may, therefore, at once state this distinction by using the adjectives which we habitually apply as expressing the natural opposition between the two—*living* spirit and *dead* matter. These terms express our current impression of the opposition between spirit and matter with sufficient accuracy, and considered only from the point of view of outward appearances this impression is no doubt correct. The general consensus of mankind is right in trusting the evidence of our senses, and any system which tells us that we are not to do so will never obtain a permanent footing in a sane and healthy community. There is nothing wrong in the evidence conveyed to a healthy mind by the senses of a healthy body, but the point where error creeps in is when we come to judge of the meaning of this testimony. We are accustomed to judge only by external appearances and by certain limited significances which we attach to words; but when we begin to enquire into the real meaning of our words and to analyse the causes which give rise to the appearances, we find our old notions gradually falling off from us, until at last we wake up to the fact that we are living in an entirely different world to that we formerly recognized. The old limited mode of thought has imperceptibly slipped away, and we discover that we have stepped out into a new order of things where all is liberty and life. This is the work of an enlightened intelligence resulting from persistent determination to discover what truth really is irrespective of any preconceived notions from whatever source derived, the determination to think honestly for ourselves instead of endeavouring to get our thinking done for us. Let us then commence by enquiring what we really mean by the livingness which we attribute to spirit and the deadness which we attribute to matter.

At first we may be disposed to say that livingness consists in the power of motion and deadness in its absence; but a little enquiry into the most recent researches of science will soon show us that this distinction does not go deep enough. It is now one of the fully-established facts of physical science that no atom of what we call "dead matter" is without motion. On the table before me lies a solid lump of steel, but in the light of up-to-date science I know that the atoms of that seemingly inert mass are vibrating with the most intense energy, continually dashing hither and thither, impinging upon and rebounding from one another, or circling round like miniature solar systems, with a ceaseless rapidity whose complex activity is enough to bewilder the imagination. The mass, as a mass, may lie inert upon the table; but so far from being destitute of the element of motion it is the abode of the never-tiring energy moving the particles with a swiftness to which the speed of an express train is as nothing. It is, therefore, not the mere fact of motion that is at the root of the distinction which we draw instinctively between spirit and matter; we must go deeper than that. The solution of the problem will never be found by comparing Life with what we call deadness, and the reason for this will become apparent later on; but the true key is to be found by comparing one degree of livingness with another.   There is, of course, one sense in which the quality of livingness does not admit of degrees; but there is another sense in which it is entirely a question of degree.   We have no doubt as to the livingness of a plant, but we realize that it is something very different from the livingness of an animal. Again, what average boy would not prefer a fox-terrier to a goldfish for a pet?   Or, again, why is it that the boy himself is an advance upon the dog? The plant, the fish, the dog, and the boy are all equally *alive;* but there is a difference in the quality of their livingness about which no one can have any doubt, and no one would hesitate to say that this difference is in the degree of intelligence.   In whatever way we turn the subject we shall always find that what we call the " livingness " of any individual life is ulti-mately measured by its intelligence.   It is the posses-sion of greater intelligence that places the animal higher in the scale of being than the plant, the man higher than the animal, the intellectual man higher than the savage.   The increased intelligence calls into activity modes of motion of a higher order corre-sponding to itself.   The higher the intelligence, the more completely the mode of motion is under its con-trol; and as we descend in the scale of intelligence, the descent is marked by a corresponding increase in *automatic* motion not subject to the control of a self-conscious intelligence. This descent is gradual from the expanded self-recognition of the highest human personality to that lowest order of visible forms which we speak of as " things," and from which self-recognition is entirely absent.

We see, then, that the livingness of Life consists in intelligence—in other words, in the power of Thought; and we may therefore say that the distinctive quality of spirit is Thought, and, as the opposite to this, we may say that the distinctive quality of matter is Form. We cannot conceive of matter without form. Some form there must be, even though invisible to the physical eye; for matter, to be matter at all, must occupy space, and to occupy any particular space necessarily implies a corresponding form. For these reasons we may lay it down as a fundamental proposition that the distinctive quality of spirit is Thought and the distinctive quality of matter is Form. This is a radical distinction from which important consequences follow, and should, therefore, be carefully noted by the student.

Form implies extension in space and also limitation within certain boundaries. Thought implies neither. When, therefore, we think of Life as existing in any particular *form* we associate it with the idea of extension in space, so that an elephant may be said to consist of a vastly larger amount of living substance than a mouse. But if we think of Life as the fact of livingness we do not associate it with any idea of extension, and we at once realize that the mouse is quite as much alive as the elephant, notwithstanding the difference in size. The important point of this distinction is that if we can conceive of anything as entirely devoid of the element of extension in space, it must be present in its entire totality anywhere and everywhere—that is to say, at every point of space simultaneously. The scientific definition of time is that it is the period occupied by a body in passing from one given point in space to another, and, therefore, according to this definition, when there is no space there can be no time; and hence that conception of spirit which realizes it as devoid of the element of space must realize it as being devoid of the element of time also; and we therefore find that the conception of spirit as pure Thought, and not as concrete Form, is the conception of it as subsisting perfectly independently of the elements of time and space. From this it follows that if the idea of anything is conceived as existing on this level it can only represent that thing as being actually present here and now. In this view of things nothing can be remote from us either in time or space: either the idea is entirely dissipated or it exists as an actual present entity, and not as something that *shall* be in the future, for where there is no sequence in time there can be no future. Similarly where there is no space there can be no conception of anything as being at a distance from us. When the elements of time and space are eliminated all our ideas of things must necessarily be as subsisting in a universal here and an everlasting now. This is, no doubt, a highly abstract conception, but I would ask the student to endeavour to grasp it thoroughly, since it is of vital importance in the practical application of Mental Science, as will appear further on.

The opposite conception is that of things expressing themselves through conditions of time and space and thus establishing a variety of *relations* to other things, as of bulk, distance, and direction, or of sequence in time. These two conceptions are respectively the conception of the abstract and the concrete, of the unconditioned and the conditioned, of the absolute and the relative. They are not opposed to each other in the sense of incompatibility, but are each the complement of the other, and the only reality is in the combination of the two. The error of the extreme idealist is in endeavouring to realize the absolute without the relative, and the error of the extreme materialist is in endeavouring to realize the relative without the absolute. On the one side the mistake is in trying to realize an inside without an outside, and on the other in trying to realize an outside without an inside; both are necessary to the formation of a subtantial entity.

II.

THE HIGHER MODE OF INTELLIGENCE CONTROLS THE LOWER.

WE have seen that the descent from personality, as we know it in ourselves, to matter, as we know it under what we call inanimate forms, is a gradual descent in the scale of intelligence from that mode of being which is able to realize its own will-power as a capacity for originating new trains of causation to that mode of being which is incapable of recognizing itself at all. The higher the grade of life, the higher the intelligence; from which it follows that the supreme principle of Life must also be the ultimate principle of intelligence. This is clearly demonstrated by the grand natural order of the universe. In the light of modern science the principle of evolution is familiar to us all, and the accurate adjustment existing between all parts of the cosmic scheme is too self-evident to need insisting upon. Every advance in science consists in discovering new subtleties of connection in this magnificent universal order, which already exists and only needs our recognition to bring it into practical use. If, then, the highest work of the greatest minds consists in nothing else than the recognition of an already existing order, there is no getting away from the conclusion that a paramount intelligence must be inherent in the Life-Principle, which manifests itself *as* this order; and thus we see that there must be a great cosmic intelligence underlying the totality of things.

The physical history of our planet shows us first an incandescent nebula dispersed over vast infinitudes of space; later this condenses into a central sun surrounded by a family of glowing planets hardly yet consolidated from the plastic primordial matter; then succeed untold millenniums of slow geological formation; an earth peopled by the lowest forms of life, whether vegetable or animal; from which crude beginnings a majestic, unceasing, unhurried, forward movement brings things stage by stage to the condition in which we know them now. Looking at this steady progression it is clear that, however we may conceive the nature of the evolutionary principle, it unerringly provides for the continual advance of the race. But it does this by creating such numbers of each kind that, after allowing a wide margin for all possible accidents to individuals, the race shall still continue :—

> " So careful of the type it seems
> So careless of the single life."

In short, we may say that the cosmic intelligence works by a Law of Averages which allows a wide margin of accident and failure to the individual.

But the progress towards higher intelligence is always in the direction of narrowing down this margin of accident and taking the individual more and more out of the law of averages, and substituting the law of individual selection. In ordinary scientific language this is the survival of the fittest. The reproduction of fish is on a scale that would choke the sea with them if every individual survived; but the margin of destruction is correspondingly enormous, and thus the law of averages simply keeps up the normal proportion of the race. But at the other end of the scale, reproduction is by no means thus enormously in excess of survival. True, there is ample margin of accident and disease cutting off numbers of human beings before they have gone through the average duration of life, but still it is on a very different scale from the premature destruction of hundreds of thousands as against the survival of one. It may, therefore, be taken as an established fact that in proportion as intelligence advances the individual ceases to be subject to a mere law of averages and has a continually increasing power of controlling the conditions of his own survival.

We see, therefore, that there is a marked distinction between the cosmic intelligence and the individual intelligence, and that the factor which differentiates the latter from the former is the presence of *individual* volition. Now the business of Mental Science is to ascertain the relation of this individual power of volition to the great cosmic law which provides for the maintenance and advancement of the race; and the point to be carefully noted is that the power of individual volition is itself the outcome of the cosmic evolutionary principle at the point where it reaches its highest level. The effort of Nature has always been upwards from the time when only the lowest forms of life peopled the globe, and it has now culminated in the production of a being with a mind capable of abstract reasoning and a brain fitted to be the physical instrument of such a mind. At this stage the all-creating Life-principle reproduces itself in a form capable of recognizing the working of the evolutionary law, and the unity and continuity of purpose running through the whole progression until now indicates, beyond a doubt, that the place of such a being in the universal scheme must be to introduce the operation of that factor which, up to this point, has been conspicuous by its absence—the factor, namely, of intelligent individual volition. The evolution which has brought us up to this standpoint has worked by a cosmic law of averages; it has been a process in which the individual himself has not taken a conscious part. But because he is what he is, and leads the van of the evolutionary procession, if man is to evolve further, it can now only be by his own conscious co-operation with the law which has brought him up to the standpoint where he is able to realize that such a law exists. His evolution in the future must be by conscious participation in the great work, and this can only be effected by his own individual intelligence and effort. It is a process of intelligent growth. No one else can grow for us: we must each grow for ourselves; and this intelligent growth consists in our increasing recognition of the universal law, which has brought us as far as we have yet got, and of our own individual relation to that law, based upon the fact that we ourselves are the most advanced product of it. It is a great maxim that Nature obeys us precisely in proportion as we first obey Nature. Let the electrician try to go counter to the principle that electricity must always pass from a higher to a lower potential and he will effect nothing; but let him submit in all things to this one fundamental law, and he can make whatever particular applications of electrical power he will.

These considerations show us that what differentiates the higher from the lower degree of intelligence is the recognition of its own self-hood, and the more intelligent that recognition is, the greater will be the power. The lower degree of self-recognition is that which only realizes itself as an entity separate from all other entities, as the *ego* distinguished from the *non-ego*. But the higher degree of self-recognition is that which, realizing its own spiritual nature, sees in all other forms, not so much the *non-ego*, or that which is not itself, as the *alter-ego,* or that which is itself in a different mode of expression. Now, it is this higher degree of self-recognition that is the power by which the Mental Scientist produces his results. For this reason it is imperative that he should clearly understand the difference between Form and Being; that the one is the mode of the relative and the mark of subjection to conditions, and that the other is the truth of the absolute and is that which controls conditions.

Now this higher recognition of self as an individualization of pure spirit must of necessity control all modes of spirit which have not yet reached the same level of self-recognition. These lower modes of spirit are in bondage to the law of their own being because they do not know the law; and, therefore, the individual who has attained to this knowledge can control them through that law. But to understand this we must inquire a little further into the nature of spirit. I have already shown that the grand scale of adaptation and adjustment of all parts of the cosmic scheme to one another exhibits the presence *somewhere* of a marvellous intelligence underlying the whole, and the question is, where is this intelligence to be found? Ultimately we can only conceive of it as inherent in some primordial substance which is the root of all those grosser modes of matter which are known to us, whether visible to the physical eye, or necessarily inferred by science from their perceptible effects. It is that power which, in every species and in every individual, becomes that which that species or individual is; and thus we can only conceive of it as a self-forming intelligence inherent in the ultimate substance of which each thing is a particular manifestation. That this primordial substance must be considered as self-forming by an inherent intelligence abiding in itself becomes evident from the fact that intelligence is the essential quality of spirit; and if we were to conceive of the primordial substance as something apart from spirit, then we should have to postulate some other power which is neither spirit nor matter, and originates both; but this is only putting the idea of a self-evolving power a step further back and asserting the production of a lower grade of undifferentiated spirit by a higher, which is both a purely gratuitous assumption and a contradiction of any idea we can form of undifferentiated spirit at all. However far back, therefore, we may relegate the original starting-point, we cannot avoid the conclusion that, at that point, spirit contains the primary substance in itself, which brings us back to the common statement that it made everything out of nothing. We thus find two factors to the making of all things, Spirit and—Nothing; and the addition of Nothing to Spirit leaves *only* spirit: $x + o = x$.

From these considerations we see that the ultimate foundation of every form of matter is spirit, and hence that a universal intelligence subsists throughout Nature inherent in every one of its manifestations. But this cryptic intelligence does not belong to the particular *form* excepting in the measure in which it is physically fitted for its concentration into self-recognizing individuality: it lies hidden in that primordial substance of which the visible form is a grosser manifestation. This primordial substance is a philosophical necessity, and we can only picture it to ourselves as something infinitely finer than the atoms which are themselves a philosophical inference of physical science: still, for want of a better word, we may conveniently speak of this primary intelligence inherent in the very substance of things as the Atomic Intelligence. The term may, perhaps, be open to some objections, but it will serve our present purpose as distinguishing *this* mode of spirit's intelligence from that of the opposite pole, or Individual Intelligence. This distinction should be carefully noted because it is by the response of the atomic intelligence to the individual intelligence that thought-power is able to produce results on the material plane, as in the cure of disease by mental treatment, and the like. Intelligence manifests itself by responsiveness, and the whole action of the cosmic mind in bringing the evolutionary process from its first beginnings up to its present human stage is nothing else but a continual intelligent response to the demand which each stage in the progress has made for an adjustment between itself and its environment. Since, then, we have recognized the presence of a universal intelligence permeating all things, we must also recognize a corresponding responsiveness hidden deep down in their nature and ready to be called into action when appealed to. All mental treatment depends on this responsiveness of spirit in its lower degrees to higher degrees of itself. It is here that the difference between the mental scientist and the uninstructed person comes in; the former knows of this responsiveness and makes use of it, and the latter cannot use it because he does not know it.

III.

THE UNITY OF THE SPIRIT.

WE have now paved the way for understanding what is meant by " the unity of the spirit." In the first conception of spirit as the underlying origin of all things we see a universal substance which, at this stage, is not differentiated into any specific forms. This is not a question of some bygone time, but subsists at every moment of all time in the *innermost* nature of all being; and when we see this, we see that the division between one specific form and another has below it a deep essential unity, which acts as the supporter of all the several forms of individuality arising out of it. And as our thought penetrates deeper into the nature of this all-producing spiritual substance we see that it cannot be limited to any one portion of space, but must be limitless as space itself, and that the idea of any portion of space where it is not is inconceivable. It is one of those intuitive perceptions from which the human mind can never get away that this primordial, all-generating living spirit must be commensurate with infinitude, and we can therefore never think of it otherwise than as universal or infinite. Now it is a mathematical

17

truth that the infinite must be a unity. You cannot have two infinites, for then neither would be infinite, each would be limited by the other, nor can you split the infinite up into fractions. The infinite is mathematically essential unity. This is a point on which too much stress cannot be laid, for there follow from it the most important consequences. Unity, as such, can be neither multiplied nor divided, for either operation destroys the unity. By multiplying, we produce a plurality of units of the same scale as the original; and by dividing, we produce a plurality of units of a smaller scale; and a plurality of units is not unity but multiplicity. Therefore if we would penetrate below the outward nature of the individual to that innermost principle of his being from which his individuality takes its rise, we can do so only by passing beyond the conception of individual existence into that of the unity of universal being. This may appear to be a merely philosophical abstraction, but the student who would produce practical results must realize that these abstract generalizations are the foundation of the practical work he is going to do.

Now the great fact to be recognized about a unity is that, *because* it is a single unit, wherever it is at all the *whole* of it must be. The moment we allow our mind to wander off to the idea of extension in space and say that one part of the unit is here and another there, we have descended from the idea of unity into that of parts or fractions of a single unit, which is to pass into the idea of a multiplicity of smaller units, and in that case we are dealing with the relative, or the relation subsisting between two or more entities which are therefore *limited by each other,* and so have passed out of the region of simple unity which is the absolute. It is, therefore, a mathematical necessity that, because the originating Life-principle is infinite, it is a single unit, and consequently, wherever it is at all, the *whole* of it must be present. But because it is *infinite,* or limitless, it is everywhere, and therefore it follows that the *whole* of spirit must be present at every point in space at the same moment. Spirit is thus omnipresent *in its entirety,* and it is accordingly logically correct that at every moment of time *all* spirit is concentrated at any point in space that we may choose to fix our thought upon. This is the fundamental fact of all being, and it is for this reason that I have prepared the way for it by laying down the relation between spirit and matter as that between idea and form, on the one hand the absolute from which the elements of time and space are entirely absent, and on the other the relative which is entirely dependent on those elements. This great fact is that pure spirit continually subsists in the absolute, whether in a corporeal body or not; and from it all the phenomena of being flow, whether on the mental plane or the physical. The knowledge of this fact regarding spirit is the basis of all conscious spiritual operation, and therefore in proportion to our increasing recognition of it our power of producing outward visible results by the action of our thought will grow. The whole is greater than its part, and therefore, if, by our recognition of this unity, we can concentrate *all* spirit into any given point at any moment, we thereby include any individualization of it that we may wish to deal with. The practical importance of this conclusion is too obvious to need enlarging upon.

Pure spirit is the Life-principle considered apart from the matrix in which it takes relation to time and space in a particular form. In this aspect it is pure intelligence undifferentiated into individuality. As pure intelligence it is infinite responsiveness and susceptibility. As devoid of relation to time and space it is devoid of individual personality. It is, therefore, in this aspect a purely impersonal element upon which, by reason of its inherent intelligence and susceptibility, we can impress any recognition of personality that we will. These are the great facts that the mental scientist works with, and the student will do well to ponder deeply on their significance and on the responsibilities which their realization must necessarily carry with it.

IV.

SUBJECTIVE AND OBJECTIVE MIND.

UP to this point it has been necessary to lay the foundations of the science by the statement of highly abstract general principles which we have reached by purely metaphysical reasoning. We now pass on to the consideration of certain natural laws which have been established by a long series of experiments and observations, the full meaning and importance of which will become clear when we see their application to the general principles which have hitherto occupied our attention. The phenomena of hypnosis are now so fully recognized as established scientific facts that it is quite superfluous to discuss the question of their credibility. Two great medical schools have been founded upon them, and in some countries they have become the subject of special legislation. The question before us at the present day is, not as to the credibility of the facts, but as to the proper inferences to be drawn from them, and a correct apprehension of these inferences is one of the most valuable aids to the mental scientist, for it confirms the conclusions of purely *a priori* reasoning by an array of experimental instances which places the correctness of those conclusions beyond doubt.

The great truth which the science of hypnotism has brought to light is the dual nature of the human mind. Much conflict exists between different writers as to whether this duality results from the presence of two actually separate minds in the one man, or in the action of the same mind in the employment of different functions. This is one of those distinctions without a difference which are so prolific a source of hindrance to the opening out of truth. A man must be a single individuality to be a man at all, and, so, the net result is the same whether we conceive of his varied modes of mental action as proceeding from a set of separate minds strung, so to speak, on the thread of his one individuality and each adapted to a particular use, or as varied functions of a single mind: in either case we are dealing with a single individuality, and how we may picture the wheel-work of the mental mechanism is merely a question of what picture will bring the nature of its action home to us most clearly. Therefore, as a matter of convenience, I shall in these lectures speak of this dual action as though it proceeded from two minds, an outer and an inner, and the inner mind we will call the subjective mind and the outer the objective, by which names the distinction is most frequently indicated in the literature of the subject.

A long series of careful experiments by highly-trained observers, some of them men of world-wide reputation, has fully established certain remarkable differences between the action of the subjective and that of the objective mind which may be briefly stated as follows. The subjective mind is only able to reason *deductively* and not inductively, while the objective mind can do both. Deductive reasoning is the pure syllogism which shows why a third proposition must necessarily result if two others are assumed, but which does not help us to determine whether the two initial statements are true or not. To determine this is the province of inductive reasoning which draws its conclusions from the observation of a series of facts. The relation of the two modes of reasoning is that, first by observing a sufficient number of instances, we inductively reach the conclusion that a certain principle is of general application, and then we enter upon the deductive process by assuming the truth of this principle and determining what result must follow in a particular case on the hypothesis of its truth. Thus deductive reasoning proceeds on the assumption of the correctness of certain hypotheses or suppositions with which it sets out : it is not concerned with the truth or falsity of those suppositions, but only with the question as to what results must necessarily follow supposing them to be true. Inductive reasoning, on the other hand, is the process by which we compare a number of separate instances with one another until we see the common factor that gives rise to them all. Induction proceeds by the comparison of

3

facts, and deduction by the application of universal principles. Now it is the deductive method only which is followed by the subjective mind. Innumerable experiments on persons in the hypnotic state have shown that the subjective mind is utterly incapable of making the selection and comparison which are necessary to the inductive process, but will accept any suggestion, however false, but having once accepted any suggestion, it is strictly logical in deducing the proper conclusions from it, and works out every suggestion to the minutest fraction of the results which flow from it.

As a consequence of this it follows that the subjective mind is entirely under the control of the objective mind. With the utmost fidelity it reproduces and works out to its final consequences whatever the objective mind impresses upon it; and the facts of hypnotism show that ideas can be impressed on the subjective mind by the objective mind of another as well as by that of its own individuality. This is a most important point, for it is on this amenability to suggestion by the thought of another that all the phenomena of healing, whether present or absent, of telepathy and the like, depend. Under the control of the practised hypnotist the very personality of the subject becomes changed for the time being; he believes himself to be whatever the operator tells him he is: he is a swimmer breasting the waves, a bird flying in the air, a soldier in the tumult of battle, an Indian stealthily tracking his victim: in short, for the time being, he identifies himself with any personality that is impressed upon him by the will of the operator, and acts the part with inimitable accuracy. But the experiments of hypnotism go further than this, and show the existence in the subjective mind of powers far transcending any exercised by the objective mind through the medium of the physical senses; powers of thought-reading, of thought-transference, of clairvoyance, and the like, all of which are frequently manifested when the patient is brought into the higher mesmeric state; and we have thus experimental proof of the existence in ourselves of transcendental faculties the full development and conscious control of which would place us in a perfectly new sphere of life.

But it should be noted that the control must be *our own* and not that of any external intelligence whether in the flesh or out of it.

But perhaps the most important fact which hypnotic experiments have demonstrated is that the subjective mind is the builder of the body. The subjective entity in the patient is able to diagnose the character of the disease from which he is suffering and to point out suitable remedies, indicating a physiological knowledge exceeding that of the most highly trained physicians, and also a knowledge of the correspondences between diseased conditions of the bodily organs and the material remedies which can afford relief. And from this it is but a step further to those numerous instances in which it entirely dispenses with the use of material remedies and itself works directly on the organism, so that complete restoration to health follows as the result of the suggestions of perfect soundness made by the operator to the patient while in the hypnotic state.

Now these are facts fully established by hundreds of experiments conducted by a variety of investigators in different parts of the world, and from them we may draw two inferences of the highest importance: one, that the subjective mind is in itself absolutely impersonal, and the other that it is the builder of the body, or in other words it is the creative power in the individual. That it is impersonal in itself is shown by its readiness to assume any personality the hypnotist chooses to impress upon it; and the unavoidable inference is that its realization of personality proceeds from its association with the particular objective mind of its own individuality. Whatever personality the objective mind impresses upon it, that personality it assumes and acts up to; and since it is the builder of the body it will build up a body in correspondence with the personality thus impressed upon it. These two laws of the subjective mind form the foundation of the axiom that our body represents the aggregate of our beliefs. If our fixed belief is that the body is subject to all sorts of influences beyond our control, and that this, that, or the other symptom shows that such an uncontrollable influence is at work upon us, then this belief is impressed upon the subjective mind, which by the law of its nature accepts it without question and proceeds to fashion bodily conditions in accordance with this belief. Again, if our fixed belief is that certain material remedies are the only means of cure, then we find in this belief the foundation of all medicine. There is nothing unsound in the theory of medicine; it is the strictly logical correspondence with the measure of knowledge which those who rely on it are as yet able to assimilate, and it acts accurately in accordance with their belief that in a large number of cases medicine will do good, but also in many instances it fails. Therefore, for those who have not yet reached a more interior perception of the law of Nature, the healing agency of medicine is a most valuable aid to the alleviation of physical maladies. The error to be combated is not the belief that, in its own way, medicine is capable of doing good, but the belief that there is no higher or better way.

Then, on the same principle, if we realize that the subjective mind is the builder of the body, and that the body is subject to no influences except those which reach it through the subjective mind, then what we have to do is to impress *this* upon the subjective mind and habitually think of it as a fountain of perpetual Life, which is continually renovating the body by building in strong and healthy material, in the most complete independence of any influences of any sort, save those of our own desire impressed upon our own subjective mind by our own thought. When once we fully grasp these considerations we shall see that it is just as easy to externalize healthy conditions of body as the contrary. Practically the process amounts to a belief in our own power of life; and since this belief, if it be thoroughly domiciled within us, will necessarily produce a correspondingly healthy body, we should spare no pains to convince ourselves that there are sound and reasonable grounds for holding it. To afford a solid basis for this conviction is the purpose of Mental Science.

V.

FURTHER CONSIDERATIONS REGARDING SUBJECTIVE AND OBJECTIVE MIND.

AN intelligent consideration of the phenomena of hypnotism will show us that what we call the hypnotic state is the *normal* state of the subjective mind. It *always* conceives of itself in accordance with some suggestion conveyed to it, either consciously or unconsciously to the mode of objective mind which governs it, and it gives rise to corresponding external results. The abnormal nature of the conditions induced by experimental hypnotism is in the removal of the normal control held by the individual's own objective mind over his subjective mind and the substitution of some other control for it, and thus we may say that the normal characteristic of the subjective mind is its perpetual action in accordance with some sort of suggestion. It becomes therefore a question of the highest importance to determine in every case what the nature of the suggestion shall be and from what source it shall proceed; but before considering the sources of suggestion we must realize more fully the place taken by subjective mind in the order of Nature.

If the student has followed what has been said regarding the presence of intelligent spirit pervading all space and permeating all matter, he will now have little difficulty in recognizing this all-pervading spirit as universal subjective mind. That it cannot *as universal mind* have the qualities of objective mind is very obvious. The universal mind is the creative power throughout Nature; and as the originating power it must first give rise to the various *forms* in which objective mind recognizes its own individuality, before these individual minds can re-act upon it; and hence, as pure spirit or *first cause*, it cannot possibly be anything else than subjective mind; and the fact which has been abundantly proved by experiment that the subjective mind is the builder of the body shows us that the power of creating by growth from within is the essential characteristic of the subjective mind. Hence, both from experiment and from *a priori* reasoning, we may say that wherever we find creative power at work there we are in the presence of subjective mind, whether it be working on the grand scale of the cosmos, or on the miniature scale of the individual. We may therefore lay it down as a principle that the universal all-permeating intelligence, which has been considered in the second and third sections, is purely subjective mind, and therefore follows the law of subjective mind, namely that it is amenable to any suggestion, and will carry out any suggestion that is impressed upon it to its most rigorously logical consequences. The incalculable importance of this truth may not perhaps strike the student at first sight, but a little consideration will show him the enormous possibilities that are stored up in it, and in the concluding section I shall briefly touch upon the very serious conclusions resulting from it. For the present it will be sufficient to realize that the subjective mind in ourselves is *the same* subjective mind which is at work throughout the universe giving rise to the infinitude of natural forms with which we are surrounded, and in like manner giving rise *to ourselves also*. It may be called the supporter of our individuality; and we may loosely speak of our individual subjective mind as our personal share in the universal mind. This, of course, does not imply the splitting up of the universal mind into fractions, and it is to avoid this error that I have discussed the essential unity of spirit in the third section, but in order to avoid too highly abstract conceptions in the present stage of the student's progress we may conveniently employ the idea of a personal share in the universal subjective mind.

To realize our individual subjective mind in this manner will help us to get over the great metaphysical difficulty which meets us in our endeavour to make conscious use of first cause, in other words to create external results by the power of our own thought. Ultimately there can be only one first cause which is the universal mind, but because it is universal it cannot, *as universal,* act on the plane of the individual and particular. For it to do so would be for it to cease to be universal and therefore cease to be the creative power which we wish to employ. On the other hand, the fact that we are working for a specific definite object implies our intention to use this universal power in application to a particular purpose, and thus we find ourselves involved in the paradox of seeking to make the universal act on the plane of the particular. We want to effect a junction between the two extremes of the scale of Nature, the innermost creative spirit and a particular external form. Between these two is a great gulf, and the question is how is it to be bridged over. It is here, then, that the conception of our individual subjective mind as our personal share in the universal subjective mind affords the means of meeting the difficulty, for on the one hand it is in immediate connection with the universal mind, and on the other it is immediate connection with the individual objective, or intellectual mind; and this in its turn is in immediate connection with the world of externalization, which is conditioned in time and space; and thus the relation between the subjective and objective minds in the individual forms the bridge which is needed to connect the two extremities of the scale.

The individual subjective mind may therefore be regarded as the organ of the Absolute in precisely the same way that the objective mind is the organ of the Relative, and it is in order to regulate our use of these two organs that it is necessary to understand what the terms "absolute" and "relative" actually mean. The absolute is that idea of a thing which contemplates it as existing *in itself* and not in relation to something else, that is to say, which contemplates the essence of it; and the relative is that idea of a thing which contemplates it as related to other things, that is to say as circumscribed by a certain environment. The absolute is the region of causes, and the relative is the region of conditions; and hence, if we wish to control conditions, this can only be done by our thought-power operating on the plane of the absolute, which it can do only through the medium of the subjective mind. The conscious use of the creative power of thought consists in the attainment of the power of Thinking in the Absolute, and this can only be attained by a clear conception of the interaction between our different mental functions. For this purpose the student cannot too strongly impress upon himself that subjective mind, on whatever scale, is intensely sensitive to suggestion, and as creative power works accurately to the externalization of that suggestion which is most deeply impressed upon it. If then, we would take any idea out of the realm of the relative, where it is limited and restricted by conditions imposed upon it through surrounding circumstances, and transfer it to the realm of the absolute where it is not thus limited, a right recognition of our mental constitution will enable us to do this by a clearly defined method.

The object of our desire is necessarily first conceived by us as bearing some relation to existing circumstances, which may, or may not, appear favourable to it; and what we want to do is to eliminate the element of contingency and attain something which is certain in itself. To do this is to work upon the plane of the absolute, and for this purpose we must endeavour to impress upon our subjective mind the idea of that which we desire quite apart from any conditions. This separation from the elements of condition implies the elimination of the idea of *time*, and consequently we must think of the thing as already in actual existence. Unless we do this we are not consciously operating upon the plane of the absolute, and are therefore not employing the creative power of our thought. The simplest practical method of gaining the habit of thinking in this manner is to conceive the existence in the spiritual world of a spiritual prototype of every existing thing, which becomes the root of the corresponding external existence. If we thus habituate ourselves to look on the spiritual prototype as the essential being of the thing, and the material form as the growth of this prototype into outward expression, then we shall see that the initial step to the production of any external fact must be the creation of its spiritual prototype. This prototype, being purely spiritual, can only be formed by the operation of *thought,* and in order to have substance on the spiritual plane it *must* be thought of as actually existing there. This conception has been elaborated by Plato in his doctrine of archetypal ideas, and by Swedenborg in his doctrine of correspondences; and a still greater teacher has said " All things whatsoever ye pray and ask for, believe that ye *have* received them, and ye *shall* receive them." (Mark xi. 24, R.V.) The difference of the tenses in this passage is remarkable. The speaker bids us first to believe that our desire *has* already been fulfilled, that it is a thing already accomplished, and then its accomplishment *will* follow as a thing in the future. This is nothing else than a concise direction for making use of the creative power of thought by impressing upon the universal subjective mind the particular thing which we desire as an already existing fact. In following this direction we are thinking on the plane of the absolute and eliminating from our minds all consideration of conditions, which imply limitation and the possibility of adverse contingencies; and we are thus planting a seed which, if left undisturbed, will infallibly germinate into **external** fruition.

By thus making intelligent use of our subjective mind, we, so to speak, create a *nucleus,* which is no sooner created than it begins to exercise an attractive force, drawing to itself material of a like character with its own, and if this process is allowed to go on undisturbed, it will continue until an external form corresponding to the nature of the nucleus comes out into manifestation on the plane of the objective and relative. This is the universal method of Nature on every plane. Some of the most advanced thinkers in modern physical science, in the endeavour to probe the great mystery of the first origin of the world, have postulated the formation of what they call "vortex rings" formed from an infinitely fine primordial substance. They tell us that if such a ring be once formed on the minutest scale and set rotating, then, since it would be moving in pure ether and subject to no friction, it must according to all known laws of physics be indestructible and its motion perpetual. Let two such rings approach each other, and by the law of attraction, they would coalesce into a whole, and so on until manifested matter as we apprehend it with our external senses, is at last formed. Of course no one has ever seen these rings with the physical eye. They are one of those abstractions which result if we follow out the observed law of physics and the unavoidable sequences of mathematics to their necessary consequences. We cannot account for the things that we *can* see unless we assume the existence of other things which we *cannot;* and the " vortex theory " is one of these assumptions. This theory has not been put forward by mental scientists but by purely physical scientists as the ultimate conclusion to which their researches have led them, and this conclusion is that all the innumerable forms of Nature have their origin in the infinitely minute nucleus of the vortex ring, by whatever means the vortex ring may have received its initial impulse, a question with which physical science, as such, is not concerned.

As the vortex theory accounts for the formation of the inorganic world, so does biology account for the formation of the living organism. That also has its origin in a primary nucleus which, as soon as it is established, operates as a centre of attraction for the formation of all those physical organs of which the perfect individual is composed. The science of embryology shows that this rule holds good without exception throughout the whole range of the animal world, including man; and botany shows the same principle at work throughout the vegetable world. All branches of physical science demonstrate the fact that every completed manifestation, of whatever kind and on whatever scale, is started by the establishment of a nucleus, infinitely small but endowed with an unquenchable energy of attraction, causing it to steadily increase in power and definiteness of purpose, until the process of growth is completed and the matured form stands out as an accomplished fact. Now if this be the universal method of Nature, there is nothing unnatural in supposing that it must begin its operation at a stage further back than the formation of the material nucleus. As soon as that is called into being it begins to operate by the law of attraction on the material plane; but what is the force which originates the material nucleus? Let a recent work on physical science give us the answer; " In its ultimate essence, energy may be incomprehensible by us except as an exhibition of the direct operation of that which we call Mind or Will." The quotation is from a course of lectures on " Waves in Water, Air and Æther," delivered in 1902, at the Royal Institution, by J. A. Fleming. Here, then, is the testimony of physical science that the originating energy is Mind or Will; and we are, therefore, not only making a logical deduction from certain unavoidable intuitions of the human mind, but are also following on the lines of the most advanced physical science, when we say that the action of Mind plants that nucleus which, if allowed to grow undisturbed, will eventually attract to itself all the conditions necessary for its manifestation in outward visible form. Now the only action of Mind is Thought; and it is for this reason that by our thoughts we create corresponding external conditions, because we thereby create the nucleus which attracts to itself its own correspondences in due order until the finished work is manifested on the external plane. This is according to the strictly scientific conception of the universal law of growth; and we may therefore briefly sum up the whole argument by saying that our thought of anything forms a spiritual prototype of it, thus constituting a nucleus or centre of attraction for all conditions necessary to its eventual externalization by a law of growth inherent in the prototype itself.

VI.

THE LAW OF GROWTH.

A CORRECT understanding of the law of growth is of the highest importance to the student of Mental Science. The great fact to be realized regarding Nature is that it is natural. We may pervert the order of Nature, but it will prevail in the long run, returning, as Horace says, by the back door even though we drive it out with a pitchfork; and the beginning, the middle, and the end of the law of Nature is the principle of growth from a vitality inherent in the entity itself. If we realize this from the outset we shall not undo our own work by endeavouring to *force* things to become that which by their own nature they are not. For this reason when the Bible says that " he who believeth shall not make haste," it is enunciating a great natural principle that success depends on our using, and not opposing, the universal law of growth. No doubt the greater the vitality we put into the germ, which we have agreed to call the spiritual prototype, the quicker it will germinate; but this is simply because by a more realizing conception we put more growing-power into the seed than we do by a feebler conception. Our mistakes always eventually resolve themselves into distrusting the law of growth. Either we fancy we can hasten it by some exertion of our own from *without,* and are thus led into hurry and anxiety, not to say sometimes into the employment of grievously wrong methods; or else we give up all hope and so deny the germinating power of the seed we have planted. The result in either case is the same, for in either case we are in effect forming a fresh spiritual prototype of an opposite character to our desire, which therefore neutralizes the one first formed, and disintegrates it and usurps its place. The law is always the same, that our Thought forms a spiritual prototype which, if left undisturbed, will reproduce itself in external circumstances; the only difference is in the sort of prototype we form, and thus evil is brought to us by precisely the same law as good.

These considerations will greatly simplify our ideas of life. We have no longer to consider two forces, but only one, as being the cause of all things; the difference between good and evil resulting simply from the direction in which this force is made to flow. It is a universal law that if we reverse the action of a cause we at the same time reverse the effect. With the same apparatus we can commence by mechanical motion which will generate electricity, or we can commence with electricity which will gen-

erate mechanical motion; or to take a simple arith-
metical instance: if $10 \div 2 = 5$, then $10 \div 5 = 2$;
and therefore if we once recognize the power of
thought to produce any results at all, we shall see
that the law by which negative thought produces
negative results is the same by which positive thought
produces positive results. Therefore all our distrust
of the law of growth, whether shown in the anxious
endeavour to bring pressure to bear from without, or
in allowing despair to take the place of cheerful expectation, is reversing the action of the original
cause and consequently reversing the nature of the
results. It is for this reason that the Bible, which
is the most deeply occult of all books, continually
lays so much stress upon the efficiency of faith and
the destructive influence of unbelief; and in like manner, all books on every branch of spiritual science em-
phatically warn us against the admission of doubt or
fear. They are the inversion of the principle which
builds up, and they are therefore the principle which
pulls down; but the Law itself never changes, and it
is on the unchangeableness of the law that all Mental
Science is founded. We are accustomed to realize
the unchangeableness of natural law in our every day
life, and it should therefore not be difficult to realize
that the same unchangeableness of law which obtains
on the visible side of nature obtains on the invisible
side as well. The variable factor is, not the law, but

our own volition; and it is by combining this variable factor with the invariable one that we can produce the various results we desire. The principle of growth is that of inherent vitality in the seed itself, and the operations of the gardener have their exact analogue in Mental Science. We do not *put* the self-expansive vitality into the seed, but we must sow it, and we may also, so to speak, water it by quiet concentrated contemplation of our desire as an actually accomplished fact. But we must carefully remove from such contemplation any idea of a strenuous effort on our part to *make* the seed grow. Its efficacy is in helping to keep out those negative thoughts of doubt which would plant tares among our wheat, and therefore, instead of anything of effort, such contemplation should be accompanied by a feeling of pleasure and restfulness in foreseeing the certain accomplishment of our desires. This is that making our requests known to God *with thanksgiving* which St. Paul recommends, and it has its reason in that perfect wholeness of the Law of Being which only needs our recognition of it to be used by us to any extent we wish.

Some people possess the power of visualization, or making mental pictures of things, in a greater degree than others, and by such this faculty may advantageously be employed to facilitate their realization of the working of the Law. But those who do not possess this faculty in any marked degree, need not be discouraged by their want of it, for visualization is not the only way of realizing that the law is at work on the invisible plane. Those whose mental bias is towards physical science should realize this **Law of Growth** as the creative force throughout all nature; and those who have a mathematical turn of mind may reflect that all solids are generated from the movement of a point, which, as our old friend Euclid tells us, is that which has no parts nor magnitude, and is therefore as complete an abstraction as any spiritual nucleus could be. To use the apostolic words, we are dealing with the substance of things not seen, and we have to attain that habit of mind by which we shall see its reality and feel that we are mentally manipulating the only substance there ultimately is, and of which all visible things are only different modes. We must therefore regard our mental creations as spiritual realities and then implicitly trust the Law of Growth to do the rest.

VII.

RECEPTIVITY.

In order to lay the foundations for practical work, the student must endeavour to get a clear conception of what is meant by the intelligence of undifferentiated spirit. We want to grasp the idea of intelligence apart from individuality, an idea which is rather apt to elude us until we grow accustomed to it. It is the failure to realize this quality of spirit that has given rise to all the theological errors that have brought bitterness into the world and has been prominent amongst the causes which have retarded the true development of mankind. To accurately convey this conception in words, is perhaps, impossible, and to attempt definition is to introduce that very idea of limitation which is our object to avoid. It is a matter of feeling rather than of definition; yet some endeavour must be made to indicate the direction in which we must feel for this great truth if we are to find it. The idea is that of realizing personality without that selfhood which differentiates one individual from another. " I am not that other because I am myself "—this is the definition of individual selfhood; but it necessarily imparts the

45

idea of limitation, because the recognition of any other individuality at once affirms a point at which our own individuality ceases and the other begins. Now this mode of recognition cannot be attributed to the Universal Mind. For it to recognize a point where itself ceased and something else began would be to recognize itself as *not* universal; for the meaning of universality is the including of *all* things, and therefore for this intelligence to recognize anything as being *outside itself* would be a denial of its own being. We may therefore say without hesitation that, whatever may be the nature of its intelligence, it must be entirely devoid of the element of self-recognition *as an individual personality* on any scale whatever. Seen in this light it is at once clear that the originating all-pervading Spirit is the grand impersonal principle of Life which gives rise to all the particular manifestations of Nature. Its absolute impersonalness, in the sense of the entire absence of any consciousness of *individual* selfhood, is a point on which it is impossible to insist too strongly. The attributing of an impossible individuality to the Universal Mind is one of the two grand errors which we find sapping the foundations of religion and philosophy in all ages. The other consists in rushing to the opposite extreme and denying the quality of personal intelligence to the Universal Mind. The answer to this error remains, as of old, in the simple question,

" He that made the eye shall He not see? He that planted the ear shall He not hear?"—or to use a popular proverb, "You cannot get out of a bag more than there is in it;" and consequently the fact that we ourselves are centres of personal intelligence is proof that the infinite, from which these centres are concentrated, must be infinite intelligence, and thus we cannot avoid attributing to it the two factors which constitute personality, namely, intelligence and volition. We are therefore brought to the conclusion that this universally diffused essence, which we might think of as a sort of spiritual protoplasm, must possess all the qualities of personality without that conscious recognition of self which constitutes separate individuality: and since the word " personality " has became so associated in our ordinary talk with the idea of " individuality " it will perhaps be better to coin a new word, and speak of the personal-ness of the Universal Mind as indicating its personal *quality*, apart from individuality. We must realize that this universal spirit permeates all space and all manifested substance, just as physical scientists tell us that the ether does, and that wherever it is, there it must carry with it all that it is in its own being; and we shall then see that we are in the midst of an ocean of undifferentiated yet intelligent Life, above, below, and all around, and permeating ourselves both mentally and corporeally, and all other beings as well.

Gradually as we come to realize the truth of this statement, our eyes will begin to open to its immense significance. It means that all Nature is pervaded by an interior personalness, infinite in its potentialities of intelligence, responsiveness, and power of expression, and only waiting to be called into activity by our recognition of it. By the terms of its nature it can respond to us only as we recognize it. If we are at that intellectual level where we can see nothing but chance governing the world, then this underlying universal mind will present to us nothing but a fortuitous confluence of forces without any intelligible order. If we are sufficiently advanced to see that such a confluence could only produce a chaos, and not a cosmos, then our conceptions expand to the idea of universal Law, and we find *this* to be the nature of the all-underlying principle. We have made an immense advance from the realm of mere accident into a world where there are definite principles on which we can calculate with certainty *when we know them.* But here is the crucial point. The laws of the universe are there, but we are ignorant of them, and only through experience gained by repeated failures can we get any insight into the laws with which we have to deal. How painful each step and how slow the progress! Æons upon æons would not suffice to grasp all the laws of the universe in their totality, not in the visible world only, but also in the world of the unseen; each failure to know the true law implies suffering arising from our ignorant breach of it; and thus, since Nature is infinite, we are met by the paradox that we must in some way contrive to compass the knowledge of the infinite with our individual intelligence, and we must perform a pilgrimage along an unceasing Via Dolorosa beneath the lash of the inexorable Law until we find the solution to the problem. But it will be asked, May we not go on until at last we attain the possession of all knowledge? People do not realize what is meant by " the infinite," or they would not ask such questions. The infinite is that which is limitless and exhaustless. Imagine the vastest capacity you will, and having filled it with the infinite, what remains of the infinite is just as infinite as before. To the mathematician this may be put very clearly. Raise x to any power you will, and however vast may be the disparity between it and the lower powers of x, both are equally incommensurate with x^n. The universal reign of Law is a magnificent truth; it is one of the two great pillars of the universe symbolized by the two pillars that stood at the entrance to Solomon's temple: it is Jachin, but Jachin must be equilibriated by Boaz.

It is an enduring truth, which can never be altered, that every infraction of the Law of Nature must carry its punitive consequences with it. We can never get beyond the range of cause and effect. There is no escaping from the law of punishment, except by knowledge. If we know a law of Nature and work with it, we shall find it our unfailing friend, ever ready to serve us, and never rebuking us for past failures; but if we ignorantly or wilfully transgress it, it is our implacable enemy, until we again become obedient to it; and therefore the only redemption from perpetual pain and servitude is by a self-expansion which can grasp infinitude itself. How is this to be accomplished? By our progress to that kind and degree of intelligence by which we realize the inherent *personalness* of the divine all-pervading Life, which is at once the Law and the Substance of all that is. Well said the Jewish rabbis of old, "The Law is a Person." When we once realize that the universal Life and the universal Law are one with the universal Personalness, then we have established the pillar Boaz as the needed complement to Jachin; and when we find the common point in which these two unite, we have raised the Royal Arch through which we may triumphantly enter the Temple. We must dissociate the Universal Personalness from every conception of individuality. The universal can never be the individual: that would be a contradiction in terms. But because the universal personalness is the root of all individual personalities, it finds its highest expression in response to those who realize its personal nature. And it is this recognition that solves the seemingly insoluble paradox. The only way to attain that knowledge of the Infinite Law which will change the Via Dolorosa into the Path of Joy is to embody in ourselves a *principle* of knowledge commensurate with the infinitude of that which is to be known; and this is accomplished by realizing that, infinite as the law itself, is a universal Intelligence in the midst of which we float as in a living ocean. Intelligence without individual personality, but which, in producing us, concentrates itself into the personal individualities which we are. What should be the relation of such an intelligence towards us? Not one of favouritism: not any more than the Law can it respect one person above another, for itself is the root and support for each alike. Not one of refusal to our advances; for without individuality it can have no personal object of its own to conflict with ours; and since it is itself the origin of all individual intelligence, it cannot be shut off by inability to understand. By the very terms of its being, therefore, this infinite, underlying, all-producing Mind must be ready immediately to respond to all who realize their true relation to it. As the very principle of Life itself it must be infinitely susceptible to feeling, and consequently it will reproduce with absolute accuracy whatever conception of itself we impress upon it; and hence if we realize the human mind as that stage in the evolution of the cosmic order at which an individuality has arisen capable of expressing, not merely the livingness, but also the personalness of the universal underlying spirit, then we see that its most perfect mode of self-expression must be by identifying itself with these individual personalities.

The identification is, of course, limited by the measure of the individual intelligence, meaning, not merely the intellectual perception of the sequence of cause and effect, but also that indescribable reciprocity of *feeling* by which we instinctively recognize something in another making them akin to ourselves; and so it is that when we intelligently realize that the innermost principle of being, must by reason of its universality, have a common nature with our own, then we have solved the paradox of universal knowledge, for we have realized our identity of being with the Universal Mind, which is commensurate with the Universal Law. Thus we arrive at the truth of St. John's statement, " Ye know all things," only this knowledge is primarily on the spiritual plane. It is not brought out into intellectual statement whether needed or not; for it is not in itself the specific knowledge of particular facts, but it is the undifferentiated principle of knowledge which we may differentiate in any direction that we choose. This is a philosophical necessity of the case, for though the action of the individual mind consists in differentiating the universal into particular applications, to differentiate the *whole* universal would be a contradiction in terms; and so, because we cannot exhaust the infinite, our possession of it must consist in our power to differentiate it as the occasion may require, the only limit being that which we ourselves assign to the manifestation.

In this way, then, the recognition of the community of *personality* between ourselves and the universal undifferentiated Spirit, which is the root and substance of all things, solves the question of our release from the iron grasp of an inflexible Law, not by abrogating the Law, which would mean the annihilation of all things, but by producing in us an intelligence equal in affinity with the universal Law itself, and thus enabling us to apprehend and meet the requirements of the Law in each particular as it arises. In this way the Cosmic Intelligence becomes individualized, and the individual intelligence becomes universalized; the two became one, and in proportion as this unity is realized and acted on, it will be found that the Law, which gives rise to all outward conditions, whether of body or of circumstances, becomes more and more clearly understood, and can therefore be more freely made use of, so that by steady, intelligent endeavour to unfold upon these lines we may reach degrees of power to which it is impossible to assign any limits. The student who would understand the rationale of the unfoldment of his own possibilities must make no mistake here. He must realize that the whole process is that of bringing the universal within the grasp of the individual by raising the individual to the level of the universal and not vice-versa. It is a mathematical truism that you cannot contract the infinite, and that you *can* expand the individual; and it is precisely on these lines that evolution works. The laws of nature cannot be altered in the least degree; but we can come into such a realization of our own relation to the universal principle of Law that underlies them as to be able to press all particular laws, whether of the visible or invisible side of Nature, into our service and so find ourselves masters of the situation. This is to be accomplished by knowledge; and the only knowledge which will effect this purpose in all its measureless immensity is the knowledge of the personal element in Universal Spirit in its reciprocity to our own personality. Our recognition of this Spirit must therefore be twofold, as the principle of necessary sequence, order or Law, and also as the principle of Intelligence, responsive to our own recognition of it.

VIII.

RECIPROCAL ACTION OF THE UNIVERSAL AND INDIVIDUAL MINDS.

It must be admitted that the foregoing considerations bring us to the borders of theological speculation, but the student must bear in mind that as a Mental Scientist it is his business to regard even the most exalted spiritual phenomena from a purely scientific standpoint, which is that of the working of a universal natural Law. If he thus simply deals with the facts as he finds them, there is little doubt that the true meaning of many theological statements will become clear to him: but he will do well to lay it down as a general rule that it is not necessary either to the use or understanding of any law, whether on the personal or the impersonal side of Nature, that we should give a theological explanation of it: although, therefore, the personal quality inherent in the universal underlying spirit, which is present in all things, cannot be too strongly insisted upon, we must remember that in dealing with it we are still dealing with a purely natural power which reappears at every point with protean variety of form, whether as person, animal, or thing. In each case what it becomes to any individual is exactly measured by that individual's recognition of it. To each and all it bears the relation of supporter of the race, and where the individual development is incapable of realizing anything more, this is the limit of the relation; but as the individual's power of recognition expands, he finds a reciprocal expansion on the part of this intelligent power which gradually develops into the consciousness of intimate companionship between the individualized mind and the unindividualized source of it.

Now this is exactly the relation which, on ordinary scientific principles, we should expect to find between the individual and the cosmic mind, on the supposition that the cosmic mind is subjective mind, and for reasons already given we can regard it in no other light. As subjective mind it must reproduce exactly the conception of itself which the objective mind of the individual, acting through his own subjective mind, impresses upon it; and at the same time, as creative mind, it builds up external facts in correspondence with this conception. " Quot homines tot sententiæ ": each one externalizes in his outward circumstances precisely his idea of the Universal Mind; and the man who realizes that by the natural law of mind he can bring the Universal Mind into perfectly reciprocal action with its own, will on the one hand make it a source of infinite instruction, and on the other a source of infinite power. He will thus wisely alternate the personal and impersonal aspects respectively between his individual mind and the Universal Mind; when he is seeking for guidance or strength he will regard his own mind as the impersonal element which is to *receive personality* from the superior wisdom and force of the Greater Mind; and when, on the other hand, he is to give out the stores thus accumulated, he must reverse the position and consider his own mind as the personal element, and the Universal Mind as the impersonal, which he can therefore *direct* with certainty by impressing his own personal desire upon it. We need not be staggered at the greatness of this conclusion, for it follows necessarily from the natural relation between the subjective and the objective minds; and the only question is whether we will limit our view to the lower level of the latter, or expand it so as to take in the limitless possibilities which the subjective mind presents to us.

I have dealt with this question at some length because it affords the key to two very important subjects, the Law of Supply and the nature of Intuition. Students often find it easier to understand how the mind can influence the body with which it is so intimately associated, than how it can influence circumstances. If the operation of thought-power were confined exclusively to the individual mind this difficulty might arise; but if there is one lesson the student of Mental Science should take to heart more than another, it is that the action of thought-power is not limited to a circumscribed individuality. What the individual does is to *give direction* to something which is unlimited, to call into action a force infinitely greater than his own, which because it is in itself impersonal though intelligent, will receive the impress of his personality, and can therefore make its influence felt far beyond the limits which bound the individual's objective perception of the circumstances with which he has to deal. It is for this reason that I lay so much stress on the combination of two apparent opposites in the Universal Mind, the union of intelligence with impersonality. The intelligence not only enables it to receive the impress of our thought, but also causes it to devise exactly the right *means* for bringing it into accomplishment. This is only the logical result of the hypothesis that we are dealing with infinite Intelligence which is also infinite Life. Life means Power, and infinite life therefore means limitless power; and limitless power moved by limitless intelligence cannot be conceived of as ever stopping short of the accomplishment of its object; therefore, given the *intention* on the part of the Universal Mind, there can be no doubt as to its ultimate accomplishment. Then comes the question of intention. How do we know what the intention of the Universal Mind may be? Here comes in the element of impersonality.

It has *no intention*, because it is *impersonal*. As I have already said, the Universal mind works by a law of averages for the advancement of the race, and is in no way concerned with the particular wishes of the individual. If his wishes are in line with the forward movement of the everlasting principle, there is nowhere in Nature any power to restrict him in their fulfilment. If they are opposed to the general forward movement, then they will bring him into collision with it, and it will crush him. From the relation between them it results that the same principle which shows itself in the individual mind as Will, becomes in the universal mind a Law of Tendency; and the direction of this tendency must always be to life-givingness, because the universal mind is the undifferentiated Life-spirit of the universe. Therefore in every case the test is whether our particular intention is in this same lifeward direction; and if it is, then we may be absolutely certain that there is no intention on the part of the Universal Mind to thwart the intention of our own individual mind; we are dealing with a purely impersonal force, and it will no more oppose us by specific plans of its own than will steam or electricity. Combining then, these two aspects of the Universal Mind, its utter impersonality and its perfect intelligence, we find precisely the sort of natural force we are in want of, something which will undertake whatever we put into its hands without asking questions or bargaining for terms, and which, having undertaken our business, will bring to bear on it an intelligence to which the united knowledge of the whole human race is as nothing, and a power equal to this intelligence. I may be using a rough and ready mode of expression, but my object is to bring home to the student the nature of the power he can employ and the method of employing it, and I may therefore state the whole position thus :—Your object is not to run the whole cosmos, but to draw particular benefits, physical, mental, moral, or financial into your own or someone else's life. From this individual point of view the universal creative power has no mind of its own, and therefore you can make up its mind for it. When its mind is thus made up for it, it never abrogates its place as the creative power, but at once sets to work to carry out the purpose for which it has thus been concentrated; and unless this concentration is dissipated by the same agency (yourself) which first produced it, it will work on by the law of growth to complete manifestation on the outward plane.

In dealing with this great impersonal intelligence, we are dealing with the infinite, and we must fully realize infinitude as that which touches all points, and if it does, there should be no difficulty in understanding that this intelligence can draw together the means requisite for its purpose even from the ends of the world; and therefore, realizing the Law according to which the result can be produced, we must resolutely put aside all questioning as to the specific means which will be employed in any case. To question this is to sow that very seed of doubt which it is our first object to eradicate, and our intellectual endeavour should therefore be directed, not to the attempt to foretell the various secondary causes which will eventually combine to produce the desired result, laying down beforehand what particular causes should be necessary, and from what quarter they should come; but we should direct our intellectual endeavour to seeing more clearly the rationale of the general law by which trains of secondary causes are set in motion. Employed in the former way our intellect becomes the greatest hindrance to our success, for it only helps to increase our doubts, since it is trying to grasp particulars which at the time are entirely outside its circle of vision; but employed in the latter it affords the most material aid in maintaining that nucleus without which there is no centre from which the principle of growth can assert itself. The intellect can only deduce consequences from facts which it is able to state, and consequently cannot deduce any assurance from facts of whose existence it cannot yet have any knowledge through the medium of the outward senses; but for the same reason it can realize the existence of a *Law* by which the as yet unmanifested circumstances may be brought into manifestation. Thus used in its right order, the intellect becomes the handmaid of that more interior power within us which manipulates the unseen substance of all things, and which we may call relative first cause.

IX.

CAUSES AND CONDITIONS.

THE expression "*relative* first cause" has been used in the last section to distinguish the action of the creative principle in the *individual* mind from Universal First Cause on the one hand and from secondary causes on the other. As it exists in *us*, primary causation is the power to initiate a train of causation directed to an individual purpose. As the power of initiating a fresh sequence of cause and effect it is first cause, and as referring to an individual purpose it is relative, and it may therefore be spoken of as relative first cause, or the power of primary causation manifested by the individual. The understanding and use of this power is the whole object of Mental Science, and it is therefore necessary that the student should clearly see the relation between causes and conditions. A simple illustration will go further for this purpose than any elaborate explanation. If a lighted candle is brought into a room the room becomes illuminated, and if the candle is taken away it becomes dark again. Now the illumination and the darkness are both conditions, the one positive resulting from the presence of the light, and the other negative resulting from its absence: from this simple example we therefore see that every positive condition has an exactly opposite negative condition corresponding to it, and that this correspondence results from their being related to the *same cause*, the one positively and the other negatively; and hence we may lay down the rule that all positive conditions result from the active presence of a certain cause, and all negative conditions from the absence of such a cause. A condition, whether positive or negative, is never *primary* cause, and the *primary* cause of any series can never be negative, for negation is the condition which arises from the absence of active causation. This should be thoroughly understood as it is the philosophic basis of all those " denials " which play so important a part in Mental Science, and which may be summed up in the statement that evil being negative, or privation of good, has no substantive existence in itself. Conditions, however, whether positive or negative, are no sooner called into existence than they become causes in their turn and produce further conditions, and so on *ad infinitum*, thus giving rise to the whole train of secondary causes. So long as we judge only from the information conveyed to us by the outward senses, we are working on the plane of secondary causation and see nothing but a succession of conditions, forming part of an endless train of antecedent conditions coming out of the past and stretching away into the future, and from this point of view we are under the rule of an iron destiny from which there seems no possibility of escape. This is because the outward senses are only capable of dealing with the relations which one mode of limitation bears to another, for they are the instruments by which we take cognizance of the relative and the conditioned. Now the only way of escape is by rising out of the region of secondary causes into that of primary causation, where the originating energy is to be found before it has yet passed into manifestation as a condition. This region is to be found *within ourselves;* it is the region of pure ideas; and it is for this reason that I have laid stress on the two aspects of spirit as pure thought and manifested form. The thought-image or ideal pattern of a thing is the *first cause* relatively to that thing; it is the substance of that thing untrammelled by any antecedent conditions.

If we realize that all visible things *must* have their origin in spirit, then the whole creation around us is the standing evidence that the starting-point of all things is in thought-images or ideas, for no other action than the formation of such images can be conceived of spirit prior to its manifestation in matter. If, then, this is spirit's modus operandi for self-expression, we have only to transfer this conception from the scale of cosmic spirit working on the plane of the universal to that of individualized spirit working on the plane of the particular, to see that the formation of an ideal image by means of our thought is setting first cause in motion with regard to this specific object. There is no difference in kind between the operation of first cause in the universal and in the particular, the difference is only a difference of scale, but the power itself is identical. We must therefore always be very clear as to whether we are *consciously* using first cause or not. Note the word "consciously" because, whether consciously or unconsciously, we are always using first cause; and it was for this reason I emphasized the fact that the Universal Mind is purely subjective and therefore bound by the laws which apply to subjective mind on whatever scale. Hence we are *always* impressing some sort of ideas upon it, whether we are aware of the fact or not, and all our existing limitations result from our having habitually impressed upon it that idea of limitation which we have imbibed by restricting all possibility to the region of secondary causes. But now when investigation has shown us that conditions are never causes in *themselves*, but only the subsequent links of a chain started on the plane of the pure ideal, what we have to do is to reverse our method of thinking and regard the ideal as the real and the outward manifestation as a mere reflection which must change with every change of the object which casts it. For these reasons it is essential to know whether we are consciously making use of first cause with a definite purpose or not, and the criterion is this. If we regard the fulfilment of our purpose as contingent upon any *circumstances*, past, present, or future, we are not making use of first cause; we have descended to the level of secondary causation, which is the region of doubts, fears, and limitations, all of which we are impressing upon the universal subjective mind with the inevitable result that it will build up corresponding external conditions. But if we realize that the region of secondary causes is the region of mere reflections we shall not think of our purpose as contingent on any conditions whatever, but shall know that by forming the idea of it in the absolute, and maintaining that idea, we have shaped the first cause into the desired form and can await the result with cheerful expectancy.

It is here that we find the importance of realizing spirit's independence of time and space. An ideal, as such, cannot be formed in the future. It must either be formed here and now or not be formed at all; and it is for this reason that every teacher, who has ever spoken with due knowledge of the subject, has impressed upon his followers the necessity of picturing to themselves the fulfilment of their desires as *already accomplished* on the spiritual plane,

as the indispensable condition of fulfilment in the visi
ble and concrete.

When this is properly understood, any anxiou
thought as to the *means* to be employed in the accom
plishment of our purposes is seen to be quite unneces
sary. If the end is already secured, then it follow
that all the steps leading to it are secured also. The
means will pass into the smaller circle of our con
scious activities day by day in due order, and then we
have to work upon them, not with fear, doubt, o:
feverish excitement, but calmly and joyously, because
we *know* that the end is already secured, and that ou:
reasonable use of such means as present themselve:
in the desired direction is only one portion of a mucl
larger co-ordinated movement, the final result o
which admits of no doubt. Mental Science does no
offer a premium to idleness, but it takes all work ou
of the region of anxiety and toil by assuring the
worker of the success of his labour, if not in the pre
cise form he anticipated, then in some other stil
better suited to his requirements. But suppose, whe
we reach a point where some momentous decision ha:
to be made, we happen to decide wrongly? On the
hypothesis that the end is already secured you canno
decide wrongly. Your right decision is as much on
of the necessary steps in the accomplishment of the en
as any of the other conditions leading up to it, an
therefore, while being careful to avoid rash action

we may make sure that the same Law which is controlling the rest of the circumstances in the right direction will influence our judgment in that direction also. To get good results we must properly understand our relation to the great impersonal power we are using. It is intelligent and we are intelligent, and the two intelligencies must co-operate. We must not fly in the face of the Law by expecting it to do *for* us what it can only do *through* us; and we must therefore use our intelligence with the knowledge that it is acting *as the instrument of a greater intelligence;* and because we have this knowledge we may, and should, cease from all anxiety as to the final result. In actual practice we must first form the ideal conception of our object with the definite intention of impressing it upon the universal mind—it is this intention which takes such thought out of the region of mere casual fancies—and then affirm that our knowledge of the Law is sufficient reason for a calm expectation of a corresponding result, and that therefore àll necessary conditions will come to us in due order. We can then turn to the affairs of our daily life with the calm assurance that the initial conditions are either there already or will soon come into view. If we do not at once see them, let us rest content with the knowledge that the spiritual prototype is already in existence and wait till some circumstance pointing in the desired direction begins to show itself.

It may be a very small circumstance, but it is the direction and not the magnitude which is to be taken into consideration. As soon as we see it we should regard it as the first sprouting of the seed we have sown in the Absolute, and do calmly, and without excitement, whatever the circumstances may seem to require, and then later on we shall see that this doing will in turn lead to further circumstances in the same direction until we find ourselves conducted step by step to the accomplishment of our object. In this way the understanding of the great principle of the Law of Supply will, by repeated experiences, deliver us more and more completely out of the region of anxious thought and toilsome labour and bring us into a new world where the useful employment of all our powers, whether mental or physical, will only be an unfolding of our individuality upon the lines of its own nature, and therefore a perpetual source of health and happiness; a sufficient inducement, surely, to the careful study of the laws governing the relation between the individual and the Universal Mind.

X.

INTUITION.

WE have seen that the subjective mind is amenable to suggestion by the objective mind; but there is also an action of the subjective mind upon the objective. The individual's subjective mind is his own innermost self, and its first care is the maintenance of the individuality of which it is the foundation; and since it is pure spirit it has its continual existence in that plane of being where all things subsist in the universal here and the everlasting now, and consequently can inform the lower mind of things removed from its ken either by distance or futurity. As the absence of the conditions of time and space must logically concentrate all things into a present focus, we can assign no limit to the subjective mind's power of perception, and therefore the question arises, why does it not keep the objective mind continually informed on all points? And the answer is that it would do so if the objective mind were sufficiently trained to recognize the indications given, and to effect this training is one of the purposes of Mental Science. When once we recognize the position of the subjective mind as the supporter of the whole individual-

6   71

ity we cannot doubt that much of what we take to be the spontaneous movement of the objective mind has its origin in the subjective mind prompting the objective mind in the right direction without our being consciously aware of it. But at times when the urgency of the case seems to demand it, or when, for some reason yet unknown, the objective mind is for a while more closely *en rapport* with the subjective mind, the interior voice is heard strongly and persistently; and when this is the case we do well to pay heed to it. Want of space forbids me to give examples, but doubtless such will not be wanting in the reader's experience.

The importance of understanding and following the intuition cannot be exaggerated, but I candidly admit the great practical difficulty of keeping the happy mean between the disregard of the interior voice and allowing ourselves to be run away with by groundless fancies. The best guide is the knowledge that comes of personal experience which gradually leads to the acquisition of a sort of inward sense of touch that enables us to distinguish the true from the false, and which appears to grow with the sincere desire for truth and with the recognition of the spirit as its source. The only general principles the writer can deduce from his own experience are that when, in spite of all appearances pointing in the direction of a certain line of conduct, there is still a persistent *feeling* that it should not be followed, in the majority of instances it will be found that the argument of the objective mind, however correct on the facts objectively known, was deficient from ignorance of facts which could not be .objectively known at the time, but which were known to the intuitive faculty. Another principle is that our *very first* impression of feeling on any subject is generally correct. Before the objective mind has begun to argue on the subject it is like the surface of a smooth lake which clearly reflects the light from above; but as soon as it begins to argue from outside appearances these also throw their reflections upon its surface, so that the original image becomes blurred and is no longer recognizable. This first conception is very speedily lost, and it should therefore be carefully observed and registered in the memory with a view to testing the various arguments which will subsequently arise on the objective plane. It is however impossible to reduce so interior an action as that of the intuition to the form of hard and fast rules, and beyond carefully noting particular cases as they occur, probably the best plan for the student will be to include the whole subject of intuition in the general principle of the Law of Attraction, especially if he sees how this law interacts with that personal quality of universal spirit of which we have already spoken.

XI.

HEALING.

THE subject of healing has been elaborately treated by many writers and fully deserves all the attention that has been given to it, but the object of these lectures is rather to ground the student in those general principles on which *all* conscious use of the creative power of thought is based, than to lay down formal rules for specific applications of it. I will therefore examine the broad principles which appear to be common to the various methods of mental healing which are in use, each of which derives its efficacy, not from the peculiarity of the method, but from it being such a method as allows the higher laws of Nature to come into play. Now the principle universally laid down by all mental healers, in whatever various terms they may explain it, is that the basis of all healing is a change in belief. The sequence from which this results is as follows:—the subjective mind is the creative faculty within us, and creates whatever the objective mind impresses upon it; the objective mind, or intellect, impresses its thought upon it; the thought is the expression of the belief; hence whatever the subjective mind creates is the reproduction externally of our beliefs. Accordingly our whole object is to change our beliefs, and we cannot do this without some solid ground of conviction of the falsity of our old beliefs and of the truth of our new ones, and this ground we find in that law of causation which I have endeavoured to explain. The wrong belief which externalizes as sickness is the belief that some secondary cause, which is really only a condition, is a primary cause. The knowledge of the law shows that there is only *one* primary cause, and this is the factor which in our own individuality we call subjective or sub-conscious mind. For this reason I have insisted on the difference between placing an idea in the sub-conscious mind, that is, on the plane of the absolute and without reference to time and space, and placing the same idea in the conscious intellectual mind which only perceives things as related to time and space. Now the only conception you can have of *yourself* in the absolute, or unconditioned, is as *purely living Spirit,* not hampered by conditions of any sort, and therefore not subject to illness; and when this idea is firmly impressed on the sub-conscious mind, it will externalize it. The reason why this process is not always successful at the first attempt is that all our life we have been holding the false belief in sickness as a substantial entity in itself and thus being a primary cause, instead of being merely a negative *condition* resulting from the *ab-*

sence of a primary cause; and a belief which has become ingrained from childhood cannot be eradicated at a moment's notice. We often find, therefore, that for some time after a treatment there is an improvement in the patient's health, and then the old symptoms return. This is because the new belief in his own creative faculty has not yet had time to penetrate down to the innermost depths of the subconscious mind, but has only partially entered it. Each succeeding treatment strengthens the sub-conscious mind in its hold of the new belief until at last a permanent cure is effected. This is the method of self-treatment based on the patient's own knowledge of the law of his being.

But "there is not in all men this knowledge," or at any rate not such a full recognition of it as will enable them to give successful treatment to themselves, and in these cases the intervention of the healer becomes necessary. The only difference between the healer and the patient is that the healer has learnt how to control the less self-conscious modes of the spirit by the more self-conscious mode, while the patient has not yet attained to this knowledge; and what the healer does is to substitute his own objective or conscious mentality, which is will joined to intellect, for that of the patient, and in this way to find entrance to his sub-conscious mind and impress upon it the suggestion of perfect health.

The question then arises, how can the healer substitute his own conscious mind for that of the patient? and the answer shows the practical application of those very abstract principles which I have laid down in the earlier sections. Our ordinary conception of ourselves is that of an individual personality which ends where another personality begins, in other words that the two personalities are entirely separate. This is an error. There is no such hard and fast line of demarcation between personalities, and the boundaries between one and another can be increased or reduced in rigidity according to will, in fact they may be temporarily removed so completely that, for the time being, the two personalities become merged into one. Now the action which takes place between healer and patient depends on this principle. The patient is asked by the healer to put himself in a receptive mental attitude, which means that he is to exercise his volition for the purpose of removing the barrier of his own objective personality and thus affording entrance to the mental power of the healer. On his side also the healer does the same thing, only with this difference, that while the patient withdraws the barrier on his side with the intention of admitting a flowing-in, the healer does so with the intention of allowing a flowing-out: and thus by the joint action of the two minds the barriers of both personalities are removed and the direction of the flow of volition is determined, that is to say, it flows from the healer as actively willing to give, towards the patient as passively willing to receive, according to the universal law of Nature that the flow must always be from the *plenum* to the *vacuum*. This mutual removal of the external mental barrier between healer and patient is what is termed establishing a *rapport* between them, and here we find one most valuable practical application of the principle laid down earlier in this book, that pure spirit is present in its entirety at every point simultaneously. It is for this reason that as soon as the healer realizes that the barriers of external personality between himself and his patient have been removed, he can then speak to the sub-conscious mind of the patient as though it were his own, for both being pure spirit the *thought* of their identity *makes* them identical, and both are concentrated into a single entity at a single point upon which the conscious mind of the healer can be brought to bear, according to the universal principle of the control of the subjective mind by the objective mind through suggestion. It is for this reason I have insisted on the distinction between *pure* spirit, or spirit conceived of apart from extension in any matrix and the conception of it as so extended. If we concentrate our mind upon the diseased condition of the patient we are thinking of him as a separate personality, and are not fixing our mind upon that conception of him as pure spirit which will afford us effectual entry to his springs of being. We must therefore withdraw our thought from the contemplation of symptoms, and indeed from his corporeal personality altogether, and must think of him as a purely spiritual individuality, and as such entirely free from subjection to any conditions, and consequently as voluntarily externalizing the conditions most expressive of the vitality and intelligence which pure spirit is. Thinking of him thus, we then make mental affirmation that he shall build up outwardly the correspondence of that perfect vitality which he knows himself to be inwardly; and this suggestion being impressed by the healer's conscious thought, while the patient's conscious thought is at the same time impressing the fact that he is receiving the active thought of the healer, the result is that the patient's sub-conscious mind becomes thoroughly imbued with the recognition of its own life-giving power, and according to the recognized law of subjective mentality proceeds to work out this suggestion into external manifestation, and thus health is substituted for sickness.

It must be understood that the purpose of the process here described is to strengthen the subject's individuality, not to dominate it. To use it for domination is *inversion,* bringing its appropriate penalty to the operator.

In this description I have contemplated the case

where the patient is consciously co-operating with the healer, and it is in order to obtain this co-operation that the mental healer usually makes a point of instructing the patient in the broad principles of Mental Science, if he is not already acquainted with them. But this is not always advisable or possible. Sometimes the statement of principles opposed to existing prejudices arouses opposition, and any active antagonism on the patient's part must tend to intensify the barrier of conscious personality which it is the healer's first object to remove. In these cases nothing is so effective as *absent treatment*. If the student has grasped all that has been said on the subject of spirit and matter, he will see that in mental treatment time and space count for nothing, because the whole action takes place on a plane where these conditions do not obtain; and it is therefore quite immaterial whether the patient be in the immediate presence of the healer or in a distant country. Under these circumstances it is found by experience that one of the most effectual modes of mental healing is by treatment during sleep, because then the patient's whole system is naturally in a state of relaxation which prevents him offering any conscious opposition to the treatment. And by the same rule the healer also is able to treat even more effectively during his own sleep than while waking. Before going to sleep he firmly impresses on his subjective mind that it is to convey curative suggestion to the subjective mind of the patient, and then, by the general principles of the relation between subjective and objective mind this suggestion is carried out during all the hours that the conscious individuality is wrapped in repose. This method is applicable to young children to whom the principles of the science cannot be explained; and also to persons at a distance: and indeed the only advantage gained by the personal meeting of the patient and healer is in the instruction that can be orally given, or when the patient is at that early stage of knowledge where the healer's visible presence conveys the suggestion that something is then being done which could not be done in his absence; otherwise the presence or absence of the patient are matters perfectly indifferent. The student must always recollect that the sub-conscious mind does not have to work *through* the intellect or conscious mind to produce its curative effects. It is part of the all-pervading creative force of Nature, while the intellect is not creative but distributive.

From mental healing it is but a step to telepathy, clairvoyance and other kindred manifestations of transcendental power which are from time to time exhibited by the subjective entity and which follow laws as accurate as those which govern what we are accustomed to consider our more normal faculties; but these subjects do not properly fall within the scope of a book whose purpose is to lay down the broad principles which underlie *all* spiritual phenomena. Until these are clearly understood the student cannot profitably attempt the detailed study of the more interior powers; for to do so without a firm foundation of knowledge and some experience in its practical application would only be to expose himself to unknown dangers, and would be contrary to the scientific principle that the advance into the unknown can only be made from the standpoint of the known, otherwise we only come into a confused region of guess-work without any clearly defined principles for our guidance.

XII.

THE WILL.

THE Will is of such primary importance that the student should be on his guard against any mistake as to the position which it holds in the mental economy. Many writers and teachers insist on will-power as though that were the creative faculty. No doubt intense will-power can evolve certain external results, but like all other methods of compulsion it lacks the permanency of natural growth. The appearances, forms, and conditions produced by mere intensity of will-power will only hang together so long as the compelling force continues; but let it be exhausted or withdrawn, and the elements thus forced into unnatural combination will at once fly back to their proper affinities; the form created by compulsion never had the germ of vitality *in itself* and is therefore dissipated as soon as the external energy which supported it is withdrawn. The mistake is in attributing the creative power to the will, or perhaps I should say in attributing the creative power to ourselves at all. The truth is that man never creates anything. His function is, not to create, but to combine and distribute that which is already in being, and what we call our creations are new combinations of already existing material, whether mental or corporeal. This is amply demonstrated in the physical sciences. No one speaks of creating energy, but only of transforming one form of energy into another; and if we realize this as a universal principle, we shall see that on the mental plane as well as on the physical we never create energy but only provide the conditions by which the energy already existing in one mode can exhibit itself in another: therefore what, relatively to man, we call his creative power, is that receptive attitude of expectancy which, so to say, makes a mould into which the plastic and as yet undifferentiated substance can flow and take the desired form. The will has much the same place in our mental machinery that the tool-holder has in a power-lathe: it is not the power, but it keeps the mental faculties in that position relatively to the power which enables it to do the desired work. If, using the word in its widest sense, we may say that the imagination is the creative function, we may call the will the centralizing principle. Its function is to keep the imagination centred in the right direction. We are aiming at consciously controlling our mental powers instead of letting them hurry us hither and thither in a purposeless manner, and we must therefore understand the relation of these powers to each other for the production of external results. First the whole train of causation is started by some emotion which gives rise to a desire; next the judgment determines whether we shall externalize this desire or not; then the desire having been approved by the judgment, the will comes forward and directs the imagination to form the necessary spiritual prototype; and the imagination thus centred on a particular object creates the spiritual nucleus, which in its turn acts as a centre round which the forces of attraction begin to work, and continue to operate until, by the law of growth, the concrete result becomes perceptible to our external senses.

The business of the will, then, is to retain the various faculties of our mind in that position where they are really doing the work we wish, and this position may be generalized into the three following attitudes: either we wish to act upon something, or be acted on by it, or to maintain a neutral position; in other words we either intend to project a force, or receive a force, or keep a position of inactivity relatively to some particular object. Now the judgment determines which of these three positions we shall take up, the consciously active, the consciously receptive, or the consciously neutral; and then the function of the will is simply to maintain the position we have determined upon; and if we maintain any given mental attitude we may reckon with all certainty on the law of attraction drawing us to those correspondences which exteriorly symbolize the attitude in question. This is very different from the semi-animal screwing-up of the nervous forces which, with some people, stands for will-power. It implies no strain on the nervous system and is consequently not followed by any sense of exhaustion. The will-power, when transferred from the region of the lower mentality to the spiritual plane, becomes simply a calm and peaceful determination to retain a certain mental attitude in spite of all temptations to the contrary, knowing that by doing so the desired result will certainly appear.

The training of the will and its transference from the lower to the higher plane of our nature are among the first objects of Mental Science. The man is summed up in his will. Whatever he does by his own will is his own act; whatever he does without the consent of his will is not his own act but that of the power by which his will was coerced; but we must recognize that, on the mental plane, no other individuality can obtain control over our will unless we first allow it to do so; and it is for this reason that all legitimate use of Mental Science is towards the strengthening of the will, whether in ourselves or others, and bringing it under the control of an enlightened reason. When the will realizes its power to deal with first cause it is no longer necessary for the operator to state to himself *in extenso* all the philosophy of its action every time he wishes to use it, but, knowing that the trained will is a tremendous spiritual force acting on the plane of first cause, he simply expresses his desire with the intention of operating on that plane, and knows that the desire thus expressed will in due time externalize itself as concrete fact. He now sees that the point which really demands his earnest attention is not whether he possesses the power of externalizing any results he chooses, but of learning to choose wisely what results to produce. For let us not suppose that even the highest powers will take us out of the law of cause and effect. We can never set any cause in motion without calling forth those effects which it already contains in embryo and which will again become causes in their turn, thus producing a series which must continue to flow on until it is cut short by bringing into operation a cause of an opposite character to the one which originated it. Thus we shall find the field for the exercise of our intelligence continually expanding with the expansion of our powers; for, granted a good intention, we shall always wish to contemplate the results of our action as far as our intelligence will permit. We may not be able to see very far, but there is one safe general principle to be gained from what has already been said about causes and conditions, which is that the whole sequence always partakes of the same char-

7

acter as the initial cause: if that character is negative, that is, destitute of any desire to externalize kindness, cheerfulness, strength, beauty or some other sort of good, this negative quality will make itself felt all down the line; but if the opposite affirmative character is in the original motive, then it will reproduce its kind in forms of love, joy, strength and beauty with unerring precision. Before setting out, therefore, to produce new conditions by the exercise of our thought-power we should weigh carefully what further results they are likely to lead to; and here, again, we shall find an ample field for the training of our will, in learning to acquire that self-control which will enable us to postpone an inferior present satisfaction to a greater prospective good.

These considerations naturally lead us to the subject of concentration. I have just now pointed out that all duly controlled mental action consists in holding the mind in one of three attitudes; but there is a fourth mental condition, which is that of letting our mental functions run on without our will directing them to any definite purpose. It is on this word *purpose* that we must fix our whole attention; and instead of dissipating our energies, we must follow an intelligent method of concentration. The word means being gathered up at a centre, and the centre of anything is that point in which all its forces are equally balanced. To concentrate therefore means first to bring our minds into a condition of equilibrium which will enable us to consciously direct the flow of spirit to a definitely recognized purpose, and then carefully to guard our thoughts from inducing a flow in the opposite direction. We must always bear in mind that we are dealing with a wonderful *potential* energy which is not yet differentiated into any particular mode, and that by the action of our mind we can differentiate it into any specific mode of activity that we will; and by keeping our thought fixed on the fact that the inflow of this energy *is* taking place and that by our mental attitude we *are* determining its direction, we shall gradually realize a corresponding externalization. Proper concentration, therefore, does not consist of strenuous effort which exhausts the nervous system and defeats its own object by suggesting the consciousness of an adverse force to be fought against, and thus creating the adverse circumstances we dread; but in shutting out all thoughts of a kind that would disperse the spiritual nucleus we are forming and dwelling cheerfully on the knowledge that, because the law is certain in its action, our desire is certain of accomplishment. The other great principle to be remembered is that concentration is for the purpose of determining the *quality* we are going to give to the previously undifferentiated energy rather than to arrange the *specific circumstances* of its manifestation. *That* is the work of the creative energy itself, which will build up its own forms of expression quite naturally if we allow it, thus saving us a great deal of needless anxiety. What we really want is expansion in a certain direction, whether of health, wealth, or what not: and so long as we get this, what does it matter whether it reaches us through some channel which we thought we could reckon upon or through some other whose existence we had not suspected. It is the fact that we are concentrating energy of a particular kind for a particular purpose that we should fix our minds upon, and not look upon any specific details as essential to the accomplishment of our object.

These are the two golden rules regarding concentration; but we must not suppose that because we have to be on our guard against idle drifting there is to be no such thing as repose; on the contrary it is during periods of repose that we accumulate strength for action; but repose does not mean a state of purposelessness. As pure spirit the subjective mind never rests: it is only the objective mind in its connection with the physical body that needs rest; and though there are no doubt times when the greatest possible rest is to be obtained by stopping the action of our conscious thought altogether, the more generally advisable method is by changing the direction of the thought and, instead of centering it upon something we intend to *do,* letting it dwell quietly upon what we *are*. This direction of thought might, of course, develop into the deepest philosophical speculation, but it is not necessary that we should be always either consciously projecting our forces to produce some external effect or working out the details of some metaphysical problem; but we may simply realize ourselves as part of the universal livingness and thus gain a quiet centralization, which, though maintained by a conscious act of the volition, is the very essence of rest. From this standpoint we see that all is Life and all is Good, and that Nature, from her clearly visible surface to her most arcane depths, is one vast storehouse of life and good entirely devoted to our individual use. We have the key to all her treasures, and we can now apply our knowledge of the law of being without entering into all those details which are only needed for purposes of study, and doing so we find it results in our having acquired the consciousness of our *oneness with the whole*. This is the great secret: and when we have once fathomed it we can enjoy our possession of the whole, or of any part of it, because by our recognition we have made it, and can increasingly make it, our own. Whatever most appeals to us at any particular time or place is that mode of the universal living spirit with which at that moment we are most in touch, and realizing this, we shall draw from it streams of vital energy which will make the very sensation of livingness a joy and will radiate from us as a sphere of vibration that can deflect all injurious suggestion on whatever plane. We may not have literary, artistic, or scientific skill to present to others the results of our communings with Nature, but the joy of this sympathetic indrawing will nevertheless produce a corresponding outflow manifesting itself in the happier look and kindlier mien of him who thus realizes his oneness with every aspect of the whole. He realizes—and this is the great point in that attitude of mind which is not directed to any specific external object—that, for himself, he is, and always must be the centre of all this galaxy of Life, and thus he contemplates himself as seated at the centre of infinitude, not an infinitude of blank space, but pulsating with living being, in all of which he knows that the true essence is nothing but good. This is the very opposite to a selfish self-centredness: it is the centre where we find that we both receive from all and flow out to all. Apart from this principle of circulation there is no true life, and if we contemplate our central position only as affording us greater advantages for in-taking, we have missed the whole point of our studies by missing the real nature of the Life-principle, which is action and re-action. If we would have life enter into us, we ourselves must enter into life—enter into the spirit of it, just as we must enter into the spirit of a book or a game to enjoy it.

There can be no action at a centre only. There must be a perpetual flowing out towards the circumference, and thence back again to the centre to maintain a vital activity; otherwise collapse must ensue either from anæmia or congestion. But if we realize the reciprocal nature of the vital pulsation, and that the outflowing consists in the habit of mind which gives itself to the good it sees in others, rather than in any specific actions, then we shall find that the cultivation of this disposition will provide innumerable avenues for the universal livingness to flow through us, whether as giving or receiving, which we had never before suspected: and this action and re-action will so build up our own vitality that each day will find us more thoroughly alive than any that had preceded it. This, then, is the attitude of repose in which we may enjoy all the beauties of science, literature and art or may peacefully commune with the spirit of nature without the aid of any third mind to act as its interpreter, which is still a purposeful attitude although not directed to a specific object: we have not allowed the will to relax its control, but have merely altered its direction; so that for action and repose alike we find that our strength lies in our recognition of the unity of the spirit and of ourselves as individual concentrations of it.

XIII.

IN TOUCH WITH SUB–CONSCIOUS MIND.

THE preceding pages have made the student in some measure aware of the immense importance of our dealings with the sub-conscious mind. Our relation to it, whether on the scale of the individual or the universal, is the key to all that we are or ever can be. In its unrecognized working it is the spring of all that we can call the automatic action of mind and body, and on the universal scale it is the silent power of evolution gradually working onwards to that "divine event, to which the whole creation moves"; and by our conscious recognition of it we make it, relatively to ourselves, all that we believe it to be. The closer our *rapport* with it becomes, the more what we have hitherto considered automatic action, whether in our bodies or our circumstances, will pass under our control, until at last we shall control our whole individual world. Since, then, this is the stupendous issue involved, the question how we are to put ourselves practically in touch with the sub-conscious mind is a very important one. Now the clue which gives us the right direction is to be found in the *impersonal* quality of sub-conscious mind of which I have spoken. Not impersonal as lacking the *elements* of personality; nor even, in the case of individual subjective mind, as lacking the sense of individuality; but impersonal in the sense of not recognizing the particular external relations which appear to the objective mind to constitute its personality, and having a realization of itself quite independent of them. If, then, we would come in touch with it we must meet it on its own ground. It can see things only from the deductive standpoint, and therefore cannot take note of the inductive standpoint from which we construct the idea of our external personality; and accordingly if we would put ourselves in touch with it, we cannot do so by bringing it down to the level of the external and non-essential but only by rising to its own level on the plane of the interior and essential. How can this be done? Let two well-known writers answer. Rudyard Kipling tells us in his story of " Kim " how the boy used at times to lose his sense of personality by repeating to himself the question, *Who* is Kim? Gradually his personality would seem to fade and he would experience a feeling of passing into a grander and a wider life, in which the boy Kim was unknown, while his own conscious individuality remained, only exalted and expanded to an inconceivable extent; and in Tennyson's life by his son we are told that at times the poet had a similar experience. We come into touch

with the absolute exactly in proportion as we withdraw ourselves from the relative: they vary inversely
to each other.

For the purpose, then, of getting into touch with
our sub-conscious mind we must endeavour to think
of ourselves as pure being, as that entity which in-
teriorly supports the outward manifestation, and doing so we shall realize that the essential quality of
pure being must be good. It is in itself *pure Life,*
and as such cannot desire anything detrimental to
pure Life under whatever form manifested. Consequently the purer our intentions the more readily we
shall place ourself *en rapport* with our subjective
entity; and *a fortiori* the same applies to that Greater
Sub-conscious Mind of which our individual subjective mind is a particular manifestation. In actual
practice the process consists in first forming a clear
conception in the objective mind of the idea we wish
to convey to the subjective mind: then, when this has
been firmly grasped, endeavour to lose sight of all
other facts connected with the external personality
except the one in question, and then mentally address
the subjective mind as though it were an independent
entity and impress upon it what you want it to do or
to believe. Everyone must formulate his own way
of working, but one method, which is both simple and
effective is to say to the subjective mind, " This is
what I want you to do; you will now step into my

place and do it, bringing all your powers and intelligence to bear, and considering yourself to be none other than myself." Having done this return to the realization of your own objective personality and leave the subjective mind to perform its task in full confidence that, by the law of its nature, it will do so if not hindered by a repetition of contrary messages from the objective mind. This is not a mere fancy but a truth daily proved by the experience of increasing numbers. The facts have not been fabricated to fit the theory, but the theory has been built up by careful observation of the facts; and since it has been shown both by theory and practice that such is the law of the relation between subjective and objective mind, we find ourselves face to face with a very momentous question. Is there any reason why the laws which hold good of the individual subjective mind should not hold good of the Universal Mind also? and the answer is that there is not. As has been already shown the Universal Mind must, by its very universality, be purely subjective, and what is the law of a part must also be the law of the whole: the qualities of fire are the same whether the centres of combustion be great or small, and therefore we may well conclude these lectures by considering what will be the result if we apply what we have learnt regarding the individual subjective mind to the Universal Mind.

We have learnt that the three great facts regarding subjective mind are its creative power, its amenableness to suggestion, and its inability to work by any other than the deductive method. This last is an exceedingly important point, for it implies that the action of the subjective mind is in no way limited by precedent. The inductive method works on principles inferred from an already existing pattern, and therefore at the best only produces the old thing in a new shape. But the deductive method works according to the essence or spirit of the principle, and does not depend on any previous concrete manifestation for its apprehension of it; and this latter method of working must necessarily be that of the all-originating Mind, for since there could be no prior existing pattern from which it could learn the principles of construction, the want of a pattern would have prevented its creating anything had its method been inductive instead of deductive. Thus by the necessity of the case the Universal Mind must act deductively, that is, according to the law which has been found true of individual subjective mind. It is thus not bound by any precedent, which means that its creative power is absolutely unlimited; and since it is essentially subjective mind, and not objective mind, it is entirely amenable to suggestion. Now it is an unavoidable inference from the identity of the law governing subjective mind, whether in the individual or the universal, that just as we can by suggestion impress a certain character of personality upon the individual subjective mind, so we can, and do, upon the Universal Mind; and it is for this reason that I have drawn attention to the inherent personal *quality* of pure spirit when contemplated in its most interior plane. It becomes, therefore, the most important of all considerations with what character we invest the Universal Mind; for since our relation to it is *purely subjective* it will infallibly bear *to us* exactly that character which we impress upon it; in other words it will be to us exactly what we believe it to be. This is simply a logical inference from the fact that, as subjective mind, our primary relation to it can only be on the subjective plane, and indirectly our objective relations must also spring from the same source. This is the meaning of that remarkable passage twice repeated in the Bible, " With the pure thou wilt show thyself pure, and with the froward thou wilt show thyself froward " (Ps. xviii., 26, and II. Sam. xxii., 27), for the context makes it clear that these words are addressed to the Divine Being. The spiritual kingdom is *within* us, and as we realize it *there* so it becomes to us a reality. It is the unvarying law of the subjective life that " as a man thinketh in his heart so is he," that is to say, his inward subjective states are the only true reality, and what we call external realities are only their objective correspondences. If we thoroughly realize the truth that the Universal Mind must be to us exactly according to our conception of it, and that this relation is not merely imaginary but by the law of subjective mind must be to us an actual fact and the foundation of all other facts, then it is impossible to over-estimate the importance of the conception of the Universal Mind which we adopt. To the uninstructed there is little or no choice: they form a conception in accordance with the tradition they have received from others, and until they have learnt to think for themselves, they have to abide by the results of that tradition: for natural laws admit of no exceptions, and however faulty the traditional idea may be, its acceptance will involve a corresponding reaction upon the Universal Mind, which will in turn be reflected into the conscious mind and external life of the individual. But those who understand the law of the subject will have no one but themselves to blame if they do not derive all possible benefits from it. The greatest Teacher of Mental Science the world has ever seen has laid down sufficiently plain rules for our guidance. With a knowledge of the subject whose depth can be appreciated only by those who have themselves some practical acquaintance with it, He bids His unlearned audiences, those common people who heard Him gladly, picture to themselves the Universal Mind as a benign Father, tenderly compassionate of all and sending the common bounties of Nature alike on the evil and the good; but He also pictured It as exercising a special and peculiar care over those who recognize Its willingness to do so :—" the very hairs of your head are all numbered," and " ye are of more value than many sparrows." Prayer was to be made to the unseen Being, not with doubt or fear, but with the absolute assurance of a certain answer, and no limit was to be set to its power or willingness to work for us. But to those who did not thus realize it, the Great Mind is necessarily the adversary who casts them into prison until they have paid the uttermost farthing; and thus in all cases the Master impressed upon his hearers the exact correspondence of the attitude of this unseen Power towards *them* with their own attitude towards *it*. Such teaching was not a narrow anthropomorphism but the adaptation to the intellectual capacity of the unlettered multitude of the very deepest truths of what we now call Mental Science. And the basis of it all is the cryptic personality of spirit hidden throughout the infinite of Nature under every form of manifestation. As unalloyed Life and Intelligence it *can* be no other than good, it can entertain no intention of evil, and thus all intentional evil must put us in opposition to it, and so deprive us of the consciousness of its guidance and strengthening and thus leave us to grope our own way and fight our own battle single-handed against the universe, odds which at last will surely prove too great for us. But remember that the opposition can never be on the part of the Universal Mind, for in itself it is sub-conscious mind; and to suppose any active opposition taken on its own initiative would be contrary to all we have learnt as to the nature of sub-conscious mind whether in the individual or the universal; the position of the Universal Mind towards us is always the reflection of our own attitude. Therefore although the Bible is full of threatening against those who persist in conscious opposition to the Divine Law of Good, it is on the other hand full of promises of immediate and full forgiveness to all who change their attitude and desire to co-operate with the Law of Good so far as they know it. The laws of Nature do not act vindictively; and through all theological formularies and traditional interpretations let us realize that what we are dealing with is the supreme law of our own being; and it is on the basis of this natural law that we find such declarations as that in Ezek. xviii., 22, which tells that if we forsake our evil ways our past transgressions shall never again be mentioned to us. We are dealing with the great principles of our subjective being, and our misuse of them in the past can never make them change their inherent law of action. If our method of using them in the past has brought us sorrow, fear and trouble, we have only to fall back on the law that if we reverse the cause the effects will be reversed also; and so what we have to do is simply to reverse our mental attitude and then endeavour to act up to the new one. The sincere endeavour to act up to our new mental attitude is essential, for we cannot really think in one way and act in another; but our repeated failures to fully act as we would wish must not discourage us. It is the sincere intention that is the essential thing, and this will in time release us from the bondage of habits which at present seem almost insuperable.

The initial step, then, consists in determining to picture the Universal Mind as the ideal of all we could wish it to be both to ourselves and to others, together with the endeavour to reproduce this ideal, however imperfectly, in our own life; and this step having been taken, we can then cheerfully look upon it as our ever-present Friend, providing all good, guarding from all danger, and guiding us with all counsel. Gradually as the habit of thus regarding the Universal Mind grows upon us, we shall find that in accordance with the laws we have been considering, it will become more and more *personal* to us, and in response to our desire its inherent intelligence will make itself more and more clearly perceptible within as a power of perceiving truth far beyond any statement of it that we could formulate by merely intellectual investigation. Similarly if we think of it as a great power devoted to supplying all our needs, we

8

shall impress this character also upon it, and by the law of subjective mind it will proceed to enact the part of that special providence which we have credited it with being; and if, beyond the general care of our concerns, we would draw to ourselves some particular benefit, the same rule holds good of impressing our desire upon the Universal Subjective Mind. And if we realize that above and beyond all this we want something still greater and more enduring, the building-up of character and unfolding of our powers so that we may expand into fuller and yet fuller measures of joyous and joy-giving Life, still the same rule holds good: convey to the Universal Mind the suggestion of the desire, and by the law of relation between subjective and objective mind this too will be fulfilled. And thus the deepest problems of philosophy bring us back to the old statement of the Law :—Ask and ye shall receive, seek and ye shall find, knock and it shall be opened unto you. This is the summing-up of the natural law of the relation between us and the Divine Mind. It is thus no vain boast that Mental Science can enable us to make our lives what we will. We must start from where we are now, and by rightly estimating our relation to the Divine Universal Mind we can gradually grow into any conditions we desire, provided we first make ourselves in habitual mental attitude the person who corresponds to those conditions: for we can never get over the law of correspondence, and the externalization will always be in accord with the internal principle that gives rise to it. And to this law there is no limit. What it can do for us to-day it can do to-morrow, and through all that procession of to-morrows that loses itself in the dim vistas of eternity. Belief in limitation is the one and only thing that causes limitation, because we thus impress limitation upon the creative principle; and in proportion as we lay that belief aside our boundaries will expand, and increasing life and more abundant blessing will be ours.

But we must not ignore our responsibilities. Trained thought is far more powerful than untrained, and therefore the more deeply we penetrate into Mental Science the more carefully we must guard against all thoughts and words expressive of even the most modified form of ill-will. Gossip, tale-bearing, sneering laughter, are not in accord with the principles of Mental Science; and similarly even our smallest thoughts of good carry with them a seed of good which will assuredly bear fruit in due time. This is not mere " goodie, goodie," but an important lesson in Mental Science, for our subjective mind takes its colour from our settled mental habits, and an occasional affirmation or denial will not be sufficient to change it; and we must therefore cultivate that tone which we wish to see reproduced in our conditions whether of body, mind, or circumstance.

In these lectures my purpose has been, not so much to give specific rules of practice as to lay down the broad general principles of Mental Science which will enable the student to form rules for himself. In every walk in life, book knowledge is only a means to an end. Books can only direct us where to look and what to look for, but we must do the finding *for ourselves;* therefore, if you have really grasped the principles of the science, you will frame rules of your own which will give you better results than any attempt to follow somebody else's method, which was successful in their hands precisely because it was theirs. Never fear to be yourself. If Mental Science does not teach you to be yourself it teaches you nothing. Yourself, more yourself, and yet more yourself is what you want; only with the knowledge that the true self includes the inner and higher self which is always in immediate touch with the Great Divine Mind.

As Walt Whitman says:—" You are not all included between your hat and your boots."

The growing popularity of the Edinburgh Lectures on Mental Science has led me to add to the present edition three more sections on Body, Soul, and Spirit, which it is hoped will prove useful by rendering the principles of the inter-action of these three factors somewhat clearer.

XIV.

THE BODY.

SOME students find it difficult to realize that mental action can produce any real effect upon material substance; but if this is not possible there is no such thing as Mental Science, the purpose of which is to produce improved conditions both of body and environment, so that the ultimate manifestation aimed at is always one of demonstration upon the plane of the visible and concrete. Therefore to afford conviction of an actual connection between the visible and the invisible, between the inner and the outer, is one of the most important points in the course of our studies.

That such a connection must exist is proved by metaphysical argument in answer to the question, "How did anything ever come into existence at all?" And the whole creation, ourselves included, stands as evidence to this great truth. But to many minds merely abstract argument is not completely convincing, or at any rate it becomes more convincing if it is supported by something of a more concrete nature; and for such readers I would give a few hints as to the correspondence between the physical and the mental. The subject covers a very wide area, and the limited space at my disposal will only allow me to touch on a few suggestive points, still these may be sufficient to show that the abstract argument has some corresponding facts at the back of it.

One of the most convincing proofs I have seen is that afforded by the " biometre," a little instrument invented by an eminent French scientist, the late Dr. Hippolyte Baraduc, which shows the action of what he calls the " vital current." His theory is that this force, whatever its actual nature may be, is universally present, and operates as a current of physical vitality perpetually, flowing with more or less energy through every physical organism, and which can, at any rate to some extent, be controlled by the power of the human will. The theory in all its minutiæ is exceedingly elaborate, and has been described in detail in Dr. Baraduc's published works. In a conversation I had with him about a year ago, he told me he was writing another book which would throw further light on the subject, but a few months later he passed over before it was presented to the world. The fact, however, which I wish to put before the reader, is the ocular demonstration of the connection between mind and matter, which an experiment with the biometre affords.

The instrument consists of a bell glass, from the inside of which is suspended a copper needle by a fine silken thread. The glass stands on a wooden support, below which is a coil of copper wire, which, however, is not connected with any battery or other apparatus, and merely serves to condense the current. Below the needle, inside the glass, there is a circular card divided into degrees to mark the action of the needle. Two of these instruments are placed side by side, but in no way connected, and the experimenter then holds out the fingers of both hands to within about an inch of the glasses. According to the theory, the current enters at the left hand, circulates through the body, and passes out at the right hand, that is to say, there is an indrawing at the left and a giving-out at the right, thus agreeing with Reichenbach's experiments on the polarity of the human body.

I must confess that, although I had read Dr. Baraduc's book, " Les Vibrations Humaines," I approached the instrument in a very sceptical frame of mind; but I was soon convinced of my error. At first, holding a mental attitude of entire relaxation, I found that the left-hand needle was attracted through twenty degrees, while the right-hand needle, the one affected by the out-going current, was repelled through ten degrees. After allowing the instrument to return to its normal equilibrium I again approached it with the purpose of seeing whether a change of mental attitude would in the least modify the flow of current. This time I assumed the strongest mental attitude I could with the intention of sending out a flow through the right hand, and the result as compared with the previous one was remarkable. The left-hand needle was now attracted only through ten degrees, while the right-hand one was deflected through something over thirty, thus clearly indicating the influence of the mental faculties in modifying the action of the current. I may mention that the experiment was made in the presence of two medical men who noted the movement of the needles.

I will not here stop to discuss the question of what the actual constitution of this current of vital energy may be—it is sufficient for our present purpose that it is there, and the experiment I have described brings us face to face with the fact of a correspondence between our own mental attitude and the invisible forces of nature. Even if we say that this current is some form of electricity, and that the variation of its action is determined by changes in the polarization of the atoms of the body, then this change of polarity is the result of mental action; so that the quickening or retarding of the cosmic current is equally the result of the mental attitude whether we suppose our mental force to act directly upon the current itself or indirectly by inducing changes in the molecular structure of the body. Whichever hypothesis we adopt the conclusion is the same, namely, that the mind has power to open or close the door to invisible forces in such a way that the result of the mental action becomes apparent on the material plane.

Now, investigation shows that the physical body is a mechanism specially adapted for the transmutation of the inner or mental power into modes of external activity. We know from medical science that the whole body is traversed by a network of nerves which serve as the channels of communication between the indwelling spiritual ego, which we call mind, and the functions of the external organism. This nervous system is dual. One system, known as the Sympathetic, is the channel for all those activities which are not consciously directed by our volition, such as the operation of the digestive organs, the repair of the daily wear and tear of the tissues, and the like. The other system, known as the Voluntary or Cerebro-spinal system, is the channel through which we receive conscious perception from the physical senses and exercise control over the movements of the body. This system has its centre in the brain, while the other has its centre in a ganglionic mass at the back of the stomach known as the solar plexus, and sometimes spoken of as the abdominal brain. The cerebro-spinal system is the channel of our volitional or conscious mental action, and the sympathetic system is the channel of that mental action which unconsciously supports the vital functions of the body. Thus the cerebro-spinal system is the organ of conscious mind and the sympathetic is that of sub-conscious mind.

But the interaction of conscious and subconscious mind requires a similar interaction between the corresponding systems of nerves, and one conspicuous connection by which this is provided is the " vagus " nerve. This nerve passes out of the cerebral region as a portion of the voluntary system, and through it we control the vocal organs; then it passes onwards to the thorax sending out branches to the heart and lungs; and finally, passing through the diaphragm, it loses the outer coating which distinguishes the nerves of the voluntary system and becomes identified with those of the sympathetic system, so forming a connecting link between the two and making the man physically a single entity.

Similarly different areas of the brain indicate their connection with the objective and subjective activities of the mind respectively, and speaking in a general way we may assign the frontal portion of the brain to the former and the posterior portion to the latter, while the intermediate portion partakes of the character of both.

The intuitional faculty has its correspondence in this upper area of the brain situated between the frontal and posterior portions, and physiologically speaking, it is here that intuitive ideas find entrance. These at first are more or less unformed and generalized in character, but are nevertheless perceived by the conscious mind, otherwise we should not be aware of them at all. Then the effort of nature is to bring these ideas into more definite and usable shape, so the conscious mind lays hold of them and induces a corresponding vibratory current in the voluntary system of nerves, and this in turn induces a similar current in the involuntary system, thus handing the idea over to the subjective mind. The vibratory current which had first descended from the apex of the brain to the frontal brain and thus through the voluntary system to the solar plexus is now reversed and ascends from the solar plexus through the sympathetic system to the posterior brain, this return current indicating the action of the subjective mind.

If we were to remove the surface portion of the apex of the brain we should find immediately below it the shining belt of brain substance called the " corpus callosum." This is the point of union between the subjective and objective, and as the current returns from the solar plexus to this point it is restored to the objective portion of the brain in a fresh form which it has acquired by the silent alchemy of the subjective mind. Thus the conception which was at first only vaguely recognized is restored to the objective mind in a definite and workable form, and then the objective mind, acting through the frontal brain—the area of comparison and analysis —proceeds to work upon a clearly perceived idea and to bring out the potentialities that are latent in it.

It must of course be borne in mind that I am here speaking of the mental ego in that mode of its existence with which we are most familiar, that is as clothed in flesh, though there may be much to say as to other modes of its activity. But for our daily life we have to consider ourselves as we are in that aspect of life, and from this point of view the physiological correspondence of the body to the action of the mind is an important item; and therefore, although we must always remember that the origin of ideas is purely mental, we must not forget that on the physical plane every mental action implies a corresponding molecular action in the brain and in the two-fold nervous system.

If, as the old Elizabethan poet says, " the soul is form, and doth the body make," then it is clear that the physical organism must be a mechanical arrangement as specially adapted for the use of the soul's powers as a steam-engine is for the power of steam; and it is the recognition of this reciprocity between the two that is the basis of all spiritual or mental healing, and therefore the study of this mechanical adaptation is an important branch of Mental Science.

Only we must not forget that it is the effect and not the cause.

At the same time it is important to remember that such a thing as reversal of the relation between cause and effect is possible, just as the same apparatus may be made to generate mechanical power by the application of electricity, or to generate electricity by the application of mechanical power. And the importance of this principle consists in this. There is always a tendency for actions which were at first voluntary to become automatic, that is, to pass from the region of conscious mind into that of subconscious mind, and to acquire a permanent domicile there. Professor Elmer Gates, of Washington, has demonstrated this physiologically in his studies of brain formation. He tells us that every thought produces a slight molecular change in the substance of the brain, and the repetition of the same sort of thought causes a repetition of the same molecular action until at last a veritable channel is formed in the brain substance, which can only be eradicated by a reverse process of thought. In this way " grooves of thought " are very literal things, and when once established the vibrations of the cosmic currents flow automatically through them and thus react upon the mind by a process the reverse of that by which our voluntary and intentional indrawing from the invisible is affected. In this way are formed what we call " habits," and hence the importance of controlling our thinking and guarding it against undesirable ideas.

But on the other hand this reactionary process may be used to confirm good and life-giving modes of thought, so that by a knowledge of its laws we may enlist even the physical body itself in the building up of that perfectly whole personality, the attainment of which is the aim and object of our studies.

XV.

THE SOUL.

HAVING now obtained a glimpse of the adaptation of the physical organism to the action of the mind we must next realize that the mind itself is an organism which is in like manner adapted to the action of a still higher power, only here the adaptation is one of mental faculty. As with other invisible forces all we can know of the mind is by observing what it does, but with this difference, that since we ourselves *are* this mind, our observation is an interior observation of states of consciousness. In this way we recognize certain faculties of our mind, the working order of which I have considered at page 84; but the point to which I would now draw attention is that these faculties always work under the influence of something which stimulates them, and this stimulus may come either from without through the external senses, or from within by the consciousness of something not perceptible on the physical plane. Now the recognition of these interior sources of stimulus to our mental faculties, is an important branch of Mental Science, because the mental action thus set up works just as accurately through the physical correspondences as those which start from the recognition of external facts, and therefore the control and right direction of these inner perceptions is a matter of the first moment.

The faculties most immediately concerned are the intuition and the imagination, but it is at first difficult to see how the intuition, which is entirely spontaneous, can be brought under the control of the will. Of course, the spontaneousness of the intuition cannot in any way be interfered with, for if it ceased to act spontaneously it would cease to be the intuition. Its province is, as it were, to capture ideas from the infinite and present them to the mind to be dealt with at its discretion. In our mental constitution the intuition is the point of origination and, therefore, for it to cease to act spontaneously would be for it to cease to act at all. But the experience of a long succession of observers shows that the intuition can be trained so as to acquire increased sensitiveness in some particular direction, and the choice of the *general direction* is determined by the will of the individual.

It will be found that the intuition works most readily in respect to those subjects which most habitually occupy our thought; and according to the physiological correspondences which we have been considering this might be accounted for on the physical plane by the formation of brain-channels specially adapted for the induction in the molecular system of vibrations corresponding to the particular class of ideas in question. But of course we must remember that the ideas themselves are not caused by the molecular changes, but on the contrary are the cause of them; and it is in this translation of thought action into physical action that we are brought face to face with the eternal mystery of the descent of spirit into matter; and that though we may trace matter through successive degrees of refinement till it becomes what, in comparison with those denser modes that are most familiar, we might call a spiritual substance, yet at the end of it it is not the intelligent thinking principle itself. The criterion is in the word " vibrations." However delicately etheric the substance its movement commences by the vibration of its particles, and a vibration is a wave having a certain length, amplitude, and periodicity, that is to say, something which can exist only in terms of space and time; and as soon as we are dealing with anything capable of the conception of measurement we may be quite certain that we are not dealing with Spirit but only with one of its vehicles. Therefore although we may push our analysis of matter further and ever further back—and on this line there is a great deal of knowledge to be gained—we shall find that the point at which spiritual power or thought-force is translated into etheric or atomic vibration will always elude us. Therefore we must not attribute the origination of ideas to molec-

9

ular displacement in the brain, though, by the re-action of the physical upon the mental which I have spoken of above, the formation of thought-channels in the grey matter of the brain may tend to facilitate the reception of certain ideas. Some people are actually conscious of the action of the upper portion of the brain during the influx of an intuition, the sensation being that of a sort of expansion in that brain area, which might be compared to the opening of a valve or door; but all attempts to induce the inflow of intuitive ideas by the physiological expedient of trying to open this valve by the exercise of the will should be discouraged as likely to prove injurious to the brain. I believe some Oriental systems advocate this method, but we may well trust the mind to regulate the action of its physical channels in a manner suitable to its own requirements, instead of trying to manipulate the mind by the unnatural forcing of its mechanical instrument. In all our studies on these lines we must remember that development is always by perfectly natural growth and is not brought about by unduly straining any portion of the system.

The fact, however, remains that the intuition works most freely in that direction in which we most habitually concentrate our thought; and in practice it will be found that the best way to cultivate the intuition in any particular direction is to meditate

upon the *abstract principles* of that particular class of
subjects rather than only to consider particular cases.
Perhaps the reason is that particular cases have to do
with specific phenomena, that is with the law working under certain limiting conditions, whereas the
principles of the law are not limited by local conditions, and so habitual meditation on *them* sets our
intuition free to range in an infinitude where the conception of antecedent conditions does not limit it.
Anyway, whatever may be the theoretical explanation, you will find that the clear grasp of abstract
principles in any direction has a wonderfully quickening effect upon the intuition in that particular direction.

The importance of recognizing our power of thus
giving direction to the intuition cannot be exaggerated, for if the mind is attuned to sympathy with
the highest phases of spirit this power opens the door
to limitless possibilities of knowledge. In its highest
workings intuition becomes inspiration, and certain
great records of fundamental truths and supreme
mysteries which have come down to us from thousands of generations bequeathed by deep thinkers of
old can only be accounted for on the supposition that
their earnest thought on the Originating Spirit,
coupled with a reverent worship of It, opened the
door, through their intuitive faculty, to the most
sublime inspirations regarding the supreme truths of

the universe both with respect to the evolution of the cosmos and to the evolution of the individual. Among such records explanatory of the supreme mysteries three stand out pre-eminent, all bearing witness to the same ONE Truth, and each throwing light upon the other; and these three are the Bible, the Great Pyramid, and the Pack of Cards—a curious combination some will think, but I hope in another volume of this series to be able to justify my present statement. I allude to these three records here because the unity of principle which they exhibit, notwithstanding their wide divergence of method, affords a standing proof that the direction taken by the intuition is largely determined by the will of the individual opening the mind in that particular direction.

Very closely allied to the intuition is the faculty of imagination. This does not mean mere fancies, which we dismiss without further consideration, but our power of forming mental images upon which we dwell. These, as I have said in the earlier part of this book, form a nucleus which, on its own plane, calls into action the universal Law of Attraction, thus giving rise to the principle of Growth. The relation of the intuition to the imagination is that the intuition grasps an idea from the Great Universal Mind, in which all things subsist *as potentials*, and presents it to the imagination in its essence rather than in a definite form, and then our image-building faculty gives it a clear and definite form which it presents before the mental vision, and which we then vivify by letting our thought dwell upon it, thus infusing our own personality into it, and so providing that personal element through which the specific action of the universal law relatively to the particular individual always takes place.* Whether our thought shall be allowed thus to dwell upon a particular mental image depends on our own will, and our exercise of our will depends on our belief in our power to use it so as to disperse or consolidate a given mental image; and finally our belief in our power to do this depends on our recognition of our relation to God, Who is the source of all power; for it is an invariable truth that our life will take its whole form, tone, and color from our conception of God, whether that conception be positive or negative, and the sequence by which it does so is that now given.

In this way, then, our intuition is related to our imagination, and this relation has its physiological correspondence in the circulus of molecular vibrations I have described above, which, having its commencement in the higher or " ideal " portion of the brain flows through the voluntary nervous system, the physical channel of objective mind, returning through the sympathetic system, the physical channel of sub-

* See my " Doré Lectures."

jective mind, thus completing the circuit and being then restored to the frontal brain, where it is consciously modelled into clear-cut forms suited to a specific purpose.

In all this the power of the will as regulating the action both of the intuition and the imagination must never be lost sight of, for without such a central controlling power we should lose all sense of individuality; and hence the ultimate aim of the evolutionary process is to evolve individual wills actuated by such beneficence and enlightenment as shall make them fitting vehicles for the outflowing of the Supreme Spirit, which has hitherto created cosmically, and can now carry on the creative process to its highest stages only through conscious union with the individual; for this is the only possible solution of the great problem, How can the Universal Mind act in all its fulness upon the plane of the individual and particular?

This is the ultimate of evolution, and the successful evolution of the individual depends on his recognizing this ultimate and working towards it; and therefore this should be the great end of our studies. There is a correspondence in the constitution of the body to the faculties of the soul, and there is a similar correspondence in the faculties of the soul to the power of the All-originating Spirit; and as in all other adaptations of specific vehicles so also here, we

can never correctly understand the nature of the ve-
hicle and use it rightly until we realize the nature of
the power for the working of which it is specially
adapted. Let us, then, in conclusion briefly consider
the nature of that power.

XVI.

THE SPIRIT.

WHAT must the Supreme All-originating Spirit be in itself? That is the question before us. Let us start with one fact regarding it about which we cannot have any possible doubt—it is *creative*. If it were not creative nothing could come into existence; therefore we know that its purpose, or Law of Tendency, must be to bring individual lives into existence and to surround them with a suitable environment. Now a power which has this for its inherent nature must be a kindly power. The Spirit of Life seeking expression in individual lives can have no other intention towards them than " that they might have life, and that they might have it more abundantly." To suppose the opposite would be a contradiction in terms. It would be to suppose the Eternal Principle of Life acting against itself, expressing itself as the reverse of what it is, in which case it would not be expressing itself but expressing its opposite; so that it is impossible to conceive of the Spirit of Life acting otherwise than to the increase of life. This is as yet only imperfectly apparent by reason of our imperfect apprehension of the position, and our conse-

126

quent want of conscious unity with the ONE Eternal Life. As our consciousness of unity becomes more perfect so will the life-givingness of the Spirit become more apparent. But in the realm of principles the purely Affirmative and Life-giving nature of the All-originating Spirit is an unavoidable conclusion. Now by what name can we call such an inherent desire to add to the fulness of any individual life—that is, to make it stronger, brighter, and happier? If this is not Love, then I do not know what else it is; and so we are philosophically led to the conclusion that Love is the prime moving power of the Creating Spirit.

But expression is impossible without Form. What Form, then, should Love give to the vehicles of its expression? By the hypothesis of the case it could not find self-expression in forms that were hateful or repugnant to it—therefore the only logical correlative of Love is Beauty. Beauty is not yet universally manifested for the same reason that Life is not, namely, lack of recognition of its Principle; but, that the principle of Beauty is inherent in the Eternal Mind is demonstrated by all that is beautiful in the world in which we live.

These considerations show us that the inherent nature of the Spirit must consist in the eternal interaction of Love and Beauty as the Active and Passive polarity of Being. Then this is the Power for the working of which our soul faculties are specially adapted. And when this purpose of the adaptation is recognized we begin to get some insight into the way in which our intuition, imagination, and will should be exercized. By training our thought to habitually dwell upon this dual-unity of the Originating Forces of Love and Beauty the intuition is rendered more and more sensitive to ideas emanating from this supreme source, and the imagining faculty is trained in the formation of images corresponding to such ideas; while on the physical side the molecular structure of the brain and body becomes more and more perfectly adjusted to the generating of vibratory currents tending to the outward manifestation of the Originating Principle. Thus the whole man is brought into unison with himself and with the Supreme Source of Life, so that, in the words of St. Paul, he is being day by day renewed after the image of Him that created him.

Our more immediately personal recognition of the All-originating Love and Beauty will thus flow out as peace of mind, health of body, discretion in the management of our affairs, and power in the carrying out of our undertakings; and as we advance to a wider conception of the working of the Spirit of Love and Beauty in its infinite possibilities, so our intuition will find a wider scope and our field of activity will expand along with it—in a word we shall discover that our individuality is growing, and that we are becoming more truly ourselves than we ever were before.

The question of the specific lines on which the individual may be most perfectly trained into such recognition of his true relation to the All-embracing Spirit of Life is therefore of supreme importance, but it is also of such magnitude that even to briefly sketch its broad outlines would require a volume to itself, and I will therefore not attempt to enter upon it here, my present purpose being only to offer some hints of the principles underlying that wonderful three-fold unity of Body, Soul, and Spirit which we all know ourselves to be.

We are as yet only at the commencement of the path which leads to the realization of this unity in the full development of all its powers, but others have trodden the way before us, from whose experiences we may learn; and not least among these was the illustrious founder of the Most Christian Fraternity of the Rosicrucians. This master-mind, setting out in his youth with the intention of going to Jerusalem, changed the order of his journey and first sojourned for three years in the symbolical city of Damcar, in the mystical country of Arabia, then for about a year in the mystical country of Egypt, and then for two years in the mystical country of Fez. Then, having during these six years learned all that was to be acquired in those countries, he returned to his native land of Germany, where, on the basis of the knowledge he had thus gained, he founded the Fraternity R. C., for whose instruction he wrote the mystical books M. and T. Then, when he realized that his work in its present stage was accomplished, he of his own free will laid aside the physical body, not, it is recorded, by decay, or disease, or ordinary death, but by the express direction of the Spirit of Life, summing up all his knowledge in the words,

" Jesus mihi omnia."

And now his followers await the coming of " the Artist Elias," who shall bring the Magnum Opus to its completion.

" Let him that readeth understand."

Printed in the United States
1009800002B